"Allport deploys good old _____ nd knowledge . . . [and] scours some pretty scientific terrain in prose that is not just splendid, but inviting and clarifying. . . . Heady, roiling, gutsy stuff, which Allport handles with aplomb. It is a wondrous dance, this parent-child two-step, and Allport perfectly catches the magic nature of the bond." —*KIRKUS REVIEW*, starred

"We have needed this book for a long time; the niche that *A Natural History of Parenting* fills is actually a continental divide [and] . . . in addressing this void, Ms. Allport brings invaluable attributes: a broad foundation in animal behavior, an enviable scientific skepticism, and a delicious, at times humorous, mix of epidemiologic detachment and intense personal concern. Above all, she has a deft, fluid writing style that allows her to cut in and out of the complex behaviors of the winged, four-footed and primate worlds with the captivated reader in eager pursuit." —NICHOLAS CUNNINGHAM, M.D.,
director of the Division of General Pediatrics,
College of Physicians and Surgeons of Columbia University

"*A Natural History of Parenting* enjoys the same broad treatment and sense of humor found in the best of David Attenborough's programs. The author is to be commended for making one of the hottest topics in evolution and ecology accessible to anyone who owns an aquarium, bird house, pregnant pet, or just a pair of binoculars. The complaints of human fathers pale when compared with the sheer economics and resources spent on raising either baby sticklebacks or pipefish." —Peter Bernhardt, author of *Natural Affairs*
and *Wily Violets and Underground Orchids*

"*A Natural History of Parenting* is a well-researched, extremely informative, and authoritative book that conveys an important message and is written with style. This is the century of biology, and Allport goes far beyond the old one-sided behaviorist theories and focuses through the powerful lens of biology. Indeed, this is so well done that I would recommend it as important reading material in a course on behavior, but it is also for anyone who is curious about the world, especially if they are a parent or plan to be one." —Bernd Heinrich, professor of biology at the University of Vermont,
and author of *A Year in the Maine Woods*

"This enchantingly written, thoroughly researched book enriched my appreciation of parenthood—including my own—in all its astonishing variety." —John Horgan, senior writer at *Scientific American*
and author of *The End of Science*

"Anyone who has ever held a baby—or has wanted to—will find much in this delightful book to inform and entertain." —Sue Hubbell, author of *Book of Bees* and *A Country Year*

Also by Susan Allport

Sermons in Stone:
The Stone Walls of New England and New York

Explorers of the Black Box:
The Search for the Cellular Basis of Memory

A
Natural
History
of Parenting

A NATURALIST LOOKS AT PARENTING
IN THE ANIMAL WORLD AND OURS

Susan
Allport

THREE RIVERS PRESS • NEW YORK

Copyright © 1997 by Susan Allport

Published by Three Rivers Press, a division of Crown Publishers, Inc., 201 East 50th Street, New York, New York 10022. Member of the Crown Publishing Group.

Originally published in hardcover by Harmony Books, a division of Crown Publishers, Inc., 1997.

Random House, Inc. New York, Toronto, London, Sydney, Auckland
www.randomhouse.com

THREE RIVERS PRESS and colophon are trademarks of Crown Publishers, Inc.

Printed in the United States of America

Library of Congress Cataloging-in-Publication Data
Allport, Susan.
A natural history of parenting : from emperor penguins to reluctant ewes, a naturalist looks at parenting in the animal world and ours / Susan Allport.
  Originally published : New York : Harmony Books, c1997.
  Includes bibliographical reference and index.
  1. Parental behavior in animals. I. Title.
  [QL762.A58 1998]
  91.56'3—dc21   7-32812
                              CIP

ISBN 0-609-80182-1

10   9   8   7   6   5   4   3   2   1

First Paperback Edition

for my parents
and my daughters

Acknowledgments

In writing this book, I have relied greatly on the research of numerous scientists in the fields of animal behavior and human evolution. Shamelessly have I appropriated small, priceless nuggets of information that might have taken them years, even decades, of observation and fieldwork to acquire. The incredible story of parental care is really their story; I have just retold it, framing it within my own experiences of raising sheep and children, weaving together the ideas of a great many. I am, of course, deeply indebted to all those scientists and especially to Robert Trivers, Tim Clutton-Brock, Richard Dawkins, and Edward O. Wilson for their very seminal work and writings.

I am also indebted to those anthropologists, biologists, and naturalists who gave of their time to be interviewed for this book and, in particular, to Tony Gaston for our many conversations about the theory of parental care and to Jane Lancaster for her insights on the evolution of the human family. Kevin Walsh allowed me to tag behind him at the New York Aquarium, and Tom Meyer shared both his bluebird boxes and his considerable enthusiasm for bluebirds. I would also like to thank Jeff Traver for all his help with sheep over the years and Van Kozelka at the Katonah Village Library for procuring for me a constant stream of articles and books. Tony Gaston, Wendy Trevathan, Suzanne Ironbiter, and Katherine Barnwell read the book in manuscript form, offering detailed, invaluable suggestions, and I am extremely grateful to them for being so generous with their time.

I also owe very special thanks to Ginger Barber for standing by this book on its rocky road to publication, to Shaye Areheart for her terrific forward momentum and editorial instincts, and to my husband, David Howell, for being his usual, supportive, inquisitive self.

Contents

THE VIRTUE OF PARENTS IS A GREAT DOWRY.

HORACE, *ODES*

A
Natural
History
of
Parenting

The Reluctant Ewe

For ten years I'd been tending a small flock of sheep on seven acres in a town in Westchester, New York, and I had seen enough lambs being born that I thought I knew exactly what to expect. I took certain things for granted. The lamb, black and glistening, eyes closed and seemingly lifeless, as it slipped out of the ewe. The ewe's quick interest in her offspring, the wet heap in the hay beneath her. Her methodical licking of it to life. She clears the nose and mouth of mucus and dries the head to prevent loss of heat from that vulnerable part. Then she works back over the entire body, speaking to the lamb all the while with gurgling, low-pitched bleats, to which the lamb soon responds with its own, weak-at-first, high-pitched "Maaaa."

The lamb begins to wriggle about, and, in a half hour or even less, it tries to get up. The ewe may knock it down again with her vigorous licking. She may even try to hold it down with a foot. But eventually the lamb succeeds and begins its search for the teat. It is guided by smell and a few simple rules or instincts. *Move toward any large object. Place your head under any projecting surface. Once in contact with an object, thrust upwards with your head, munching and sucking on anything that touches your mouth.* The ewe does not assist the lamb in this quest, but her tendency to turn and lick it as it moves toward her (the only large object around) eventually brings the lamb in contact with her udder. There it munches and sucks on everything it encounters until it finally finds what it's looking for.

This is what I had come to expect. It didn't seem to matter whether the ewe was an experienced mother delivering her third set of twins or a maternal neophyte faced with her first lamb. The umbilical cord would break as the lamb dropped to the ground, but it would be immediately replaced by a tether just as strong, a tether made of senses— smell, taste, sight, touch, and sound—a tether that binds ewe and lamb together and synchronizes their behavior, that locks them into a tight two-step in which the needs of the lamb and the caregiving of the ewe are perfectly matched.

Last April, though, one of my yearling ewes delivered a healthy male lamb and turned all these expectations inside out.

I had never intended to breed this yearling ewe. "Children should not have children," I've said, probably much too often, to my own two girls, and I've tried to apply this principle to life in the sheep shed as well. The ewe had been born in March of the previous year, which meant that she was sexually mature in September but that she would not reach her full adult size for some time. Last November, however, when the ram we rented from an upstate sheep farmer was doggedly pursuing all of our ewes as they came into estrus, the yearling, who had been kept in a separate pen, somehow got free. By January we realized that the ram had had his way with her too.

I had already had one unusual delivery that day when the yearling delivered. A three-year-old ewe had given birth to twins—a male lamb weighing twelve pounds and a female, only four. The ewe lamb looked more like a rat, and I had visited mother and lambs often during the day to make sure she was nursing—even to the point of holding her twin brother back. The rationing appeared to be working, and that afternoon when I brought grain down for all the sheep, the pint-sized female was already catching up.

The sheep gathered at the trough as usual, butting one another to get a better position, eating quickly and noisily. The yearling was there, unaware, it seemed, of the two dark hooves protruding from her backside. Twenty minutes later, a nose was visible; twenty minutes more, a head. No longer was the yearling unaware. Now she pawed the ground, gasping and blowing through her nostrils. She lay down, chewed her cud, then rose, heavy and awkward, to paw the ground some more.

I sat on a log some fifteen feet away, waiting for the lamb to drop out so that I could treat the broken umbilical cord with iodine, then pen the two together. Thus, I was watching when, with a heavy grunt from the yearling, the lamb dropped to the ground. I was watching when, instead of turning to investigate her offspring, instead of smelling the lamb and licking the lamb, talking to the lamb and listening to the lamb, the ewe simply and quickly walked away. Without a moment's hesitation. Without a backward glance. She cared, it seemed, as much for the creature lying there on the damp ground as for one of her innumerable daily droppings. I felt as if I was watching the ovine equivalent of a teenage mother, with an unwanted, unplanned pregnancy, placing her newborn in a trash container before she headed off to school. And, of course, I was.

I picked up the lamb and hurried after the ewe, shoving the lamb under her nose to encourage her to begin licking it, knowing that if this relationship didn't take I would soon have a very time-consuming bottle lamb on my hands. She turned away and ran off, trailing the placenta behind her. I thought of all the methods that shepherds have of encouraging a ewe to adopt an orphan lamb: rubbing the orphan with afterbirth or squirting it with kerosene or the mother's milk or the ruse that Gabriel Oak and Bathsheba had used in *Far from the Madding Crowd,* draping the skin of the ewe's dead lamb over the orphan's back. But this was different. This was a mother rejecting her own lamb.

Perhaps I could appeal to even more basic instincts, I thought, and hurried inside to get a loaf of bread, which I then rubbed all over the lamb. If the ewe ate the bread—one of a sheep's favorite foods—she would be tricked into imbibing the birth fluids and, possibly, into behaving like the mother she was. I caught the ewe and penned her and her bread-encrusted offspring, but she couldn't have been less interested. The lamb played his part beautifully, bleating softly, trying to right himself, but the ewe only pawed at the gate to get out. If she wasn't pawing at the gate, she was butting at her son.

It was one of the first really warm days that we'd had, but despite the temperature outside, the lamb's mouth was growing cold. It needed to nurse. Lambs that do not stand and nurse within the first hour have a very poor chance of surviving. I tied up the ewe and held the lamb to her udder. He was quick to catch on and suckled for almost half an hour, then fell immediately to sleep. I went down to the sheep shed two more times that night and had to tie the ewe up each time so the lamb could nurse. I hoped to see some spark of a growing attachment but saw instead a furious ewe, desperate to be let out.

The next morning I didn't know what I'd find. I was surprised at how quiet the shed was as I walked toward it. No angrily baaing ewe. No hungrily bleating lamb. Had the lamb died and the ewe broken out? No, there they were, the lamb nursing vigorously, tail wagging;

the ewe standing still and allowing this most ordinary, most extraordinary of things to take place. At one point, the ewe looked as if she might turn and butt the lamb, then, at the last moment, the butt turned into a normal maternal tail-sniffing motion. She still wasn't talking to the lamb—she didn't answer his bleats with her baas—but by the end of the day that too came. The following day, I was able to let them out in the field, knowing that ewe and lamb were tethered (far more effectively than when I had the ewe tied up in the shed), and I could now relax.

Or could I? Something about that ewe, so totally lacking in everything that it would take to ensure the survival of her lamb, made me realize that I had been taking much for granted. What is this thing that we call maternal instinct? Is it instinctive? If so, why does it sometimes fail? This ewe, of course, was not the first animal mother to have walked away from her young, nor would she be the last. Lionesses are known for abandoning (or eating) their first litters; bears that have lost one cub often leave the second to starve. Birds abandon their nests under a variety of conditions. But why? Are these animals simply making mistakes? Are these the bad parents of the animal world? Or is something else going on? In the case of my yearling ewe, was she too immature to care for her lamb? But what would that mean? That she lacked the appropriate hormonal or physiological machinery? If that were so, then one night's penning wouldn't have solved the problem. No, it wasn't a lack of mother's milk that had kept the ewe from accepting her lamb. It wasn't the ewe's hormones or her physiology that was off but her parental behavior, behavior that was every bit as important to the lamb's survival as the mother's ability to mate and bear healthy young.

I didn't realize it at the time, but my unmaternal ewe had opened a small door for me into the natural world, and I—as a science writer, a part-time shepherd, a mother—was inclined to go through it and look for the answers to these questions and to the others that ensued.

Why do some animals care for their young while others bear them and then leave them to their fate? In those animals that do care, why do some rely on mothers to raise the offspring and others, fathers? Or fathers and mothers? Why is parenting a lifelong job for some animals and temporary employment for others? What, if anything, can we learn from the startling array of parental behaviors in other animals about being a human parent—a father or a mother—or about what it takes to be a good parent?

As I delved deeper and deeper into parental care, I realized that it was no coincidence that I should have seen that small door, opened, and entered it. I had been circling this subject for a long time as I struggled with the legacy of a family in which long-lasting marriages were rarer than hen's teeth and parents often put their needs ahead of whatever children they had brought into the world. Long, unexplained absences of both my parents had left their mark on me, and when it came time to have children of my own, parenting had not come easily. Sensitivity had not been high on the list of my family's most valued character traits; plus, I was filled with the dogma of the seventies, the idea that children should not interfere with one's career. Mindlessly, I headed off to my office on the day I returned from the hospital. But my daughters gradually brought me around. They, who had never learned to conceal their hurts, taught me how to mother them. They schooled me in sensitivity until, finally, I began to find that terra firma that some people are born knowing and others are raised on.

So it was a door into my past that the ewe opened, but it was also, I soon discovered, a very public door, a door that many scientists had entered in the last two decades, asking similar questions and discovering startling things about parental behavior. Ever since researchers laid out a theoretical framework for parental behavior in the early 1970s, ever since it became possible, with DNA fingerprinting, to determine the exact relationships of offspring and the adults that care for them, this has been one of the richest and most productive areas of biological research, casting endless amounts of light on the origins and evolution of parental care, and yielding such peculiar observations as the fact that the dominant females in a baboon troop almost always give birth to girls, that some animals—flamingos and bottle-nosed dolphins, for example—form day-care centers for their young, that some insects care for their young for at least three years and sometimes five.

In the end, I would find answers to my questions about my yearling ewe, but I would also find that my simple views of parents and maternal instinct had been turned upside down and inside out. I would learn a great deal more about the two-step that most ewes and lambs perform perfectly from birth to weaning, but I would also learn about our human two-step (or should it be called a three-step, since it is danced by father, mother, and child?), so different in form, tempo, and duration.

The door would take me away from my home: to bat caves in Mexico and Texas, to the New York Aquarium to observe the maternal behavior of beluga whales, to the Bird House at the Bronx Zoo to watch the hornbills, but, most of all, deep into my own backyard, where bluebirds, finches, starlings, white-tailed deer, paper wasps, bees, sheep, moles, mice, chipmunks, rabbits, and squirrels were all busy preparing and caring for their young, each in their own way—all extraordinary ways of being a parent.

II

Parenting Across the Biological Spectrum

One fall, long after the first killing frost but before the ground had frozen solid, I asked Tom Meyer, the bluebird guru in the town where I live, to help me put up some bluebird boxes. Tom, who advises people about their financial investments when he is not counseling them about bluebirds, brought over two. One was made by Beresford Proctor, a woodworker and retired banker from Mamaroneck, New York, who built more than three thousand bluebird boxes before he died in 1994; the other, a box with much less of a provenance, from Vermont. Both were simple redwood affairs. Both provided ventilation at the top and drainage at the bottom, and both lacked perches so as to discourage perching birds like the house sparrow. Both had holes exactly one and a half inches in diameter—wide enough that bluebirds could fly in and out without damaging their wings but not wide enough for starlings, the bluebird's chief competitor for nesting sites and all-round nemesis. But for a reason known only to bluebirds, Tom said, the birds seem to prefer the boxes from Vermont.

As Tom and I walked around my property looking for the right place to site the boxes, he told me what bluebirds look for in the way of a home and a neighborhood: a southeasterly exposure, so that their eggs and nestlings will get the benefit of the early-morning sun; rolling, open terrain with sparse ground cover where they can find insects; nearby trees in which they can perch and from which they can observe the box and flutter down to the ground to seize a passing spider or caterpillar. This "dropping" technique cannot be practiced just anywhere, for it requires that the birds be able to see the ground from their normal perching height of seven to thirty feet. But compared with the "hopping" technique of the American robin, for example, it is an energetically inexpensive way to feed.

I also learned why the bluebirds are so dependent upon these boxes for their survival. When Shakespeare had Hotspur proclaim in *Henry IV*, "Nay, I'll have a starling shall be taught to speak nothing but 'Mortimer,' " he could not have imagined the effect this little speech would have on North American songbirds—and particularly the bluebird. At the end of the nineteenth century, the American Acclimatization Society was founded with the goal of establishing in the United States every species of bird mentioned by the great bard. The European starling throve in its new environment, and this once-welcome guest now always wins out in competitions with the bluebird for natural nesting cavities—in trees, fences, or houses. Between

1957 and 1967, the year when ornithologists came to realize that, as long as there are starlings in America, bluebird boxes are the bluebirds' only hope, the population of eastern bluebirds was reported to have declined by over 80 percent.

But starlings are not the only reason for the bluebird's decline. Another is far more subtle and goes back thousands of years. The bluebird, with its innate preference for cleared spaces surrounded by woodlands, is the perfect settlement bird. It benefited from the opening of the eastern forest, from agriculture and all that agriculture brought with it: clearing, lumbering, fencing, orchards, pastures.

The bluebird's fortunes soared when American Indians and then Europeans began farming the Northeast, and, by the 1800s, it was one of the most common dooryard birds, frequenting almost every orchard and grove, nesting in hollow stumps and fence posts. But its fortunes fell just as fast when farms gave way to suburbs and fields to lawns, especially lawns sprayed with pesticides. Today in the Northeast, bluebirds are rare enough to be something of a status symbol, and Tom says he is always getting calls from cross homeowners asking why the So-and-Sos have bluebirds in their box and they don't. He doesn't mind, he says, as long as it means that people are putting up boxes.

Given the bluebird's preference in habitat, it wasn't surprising that Tom chose to site the boxes he had brought over in the fields where my husband and I pasture our sheep. Not only did these fields have the closely shorn, well-lit areas that bluebirds like but the edges of the fields were a tangle of bittersweet, sumac, chokecherries, and honeysuckle, vines and shrubs that my husband and I had never gotten round to clearing. Come spring, all these plants would still have some of last year's fruits on them, dried fruits that could tide the bluebirds over while they waited for the first insects to hatch. All would also bear new fruits in the summer, and during the hot months of July and August, the bluebird parents could feed berries to their nestlings to keep them from becoming dehydrated.

Beresford Proctor's box was placed in a spot where it could be seen from the kitchen window; the Vermont box, in the field next to the sheep shed. Both locations seemed to provide everything a bluebird requires, and, in less than a week, as I was bringing grain down to the sheep, I heard an unfamiliar warble against the familiar backdrop of bird sound—of chickadee, house finch, grackle, and jay. I don't have much of a memory for birdsongs, but this one stood out like a freshly painted barn, a tree suddenly in bloom.

I looked around, and there was a bluebird standing on top of the Vermont box singing as if he had just discovered a new continent. I felt, of course, vaguely virtuous, one of the chosen ones. Yet I knew enough about bluebirds by then to know how little this had to do with personal virtue, how much with the fact that our sheep field was a kind of a bluebird's Eden, a near-perfect replica of the habitat which had caused the bluebirds' population to explode in the first place. No amount of boxes will make up for the loss of the bluebird's preferred habitat, as Tom is very aware. "It's clear that bluebirds need more than lawn," he once told me, "because you simply don't find them in the suburbs."

Tom had told me that male birds sometimes inspect boxes in the fall before migrating south and that, when such an inspection occurs, occupation by a bluebird pair is bound to follow in the spring. In April, sure enough, as my five ewes started to drop their lambs amid the daffodils, I began to catch sight of bluebirds, flying through the trees like small chunks of sky. I was too busy with lambing to watch them closely, but one day I looked in the box and saw three or four long pine needles; a week or so after that the box contained a perfect cup of a nest, constructed of pine needles and dried grasses.

Then came the silent, secretive business of egg laying. No longer did the male stand on the top of the box singing poignant tunes; I hardly saw either him or the female. But day after day, a blue egg was added to the nest cup until the eggs numbered five—a normal clutch size for bluebirds. I called Tom Meyer, and he told me that it was the earliest nest he had heard about that year. He also warned me that other birds might still try to take over the box. House wrens have been known to poke holes in the bluebird's eggs, then build their messy stick nests on top (the kind of nest that was soon to fill my other, less bluebird-friendly Proctor box), and English sparrows might peck the female bluebird to death, then throw her and the eggs out of the box. He also warned of nonavian dangers—raccoons, cats, opossums, black rat snakes—and told me to coat the nest pole with carnauba car wax. As an extra precaution, I put a bell on my daughter's cat, a huntress of some repute. There was nothing left to do but wait and hope that the weather would hold so that the female bluebird could continue incubating the eggs she had laid so early in the season. If the weather turned bad, the pair might give up their nest and breeding territory and join with other bluebirds in a large flock, a behavior that would help them find food enough to ride out the inclemency.

Although there was nothing left for me to do, I found myself dreaming about bluebirds one night. In my dream, the birds were being led to their boxes by the father of one of my daughter's class-mates. A most unlikely Pied Piper of bluebirds, I thought when I awoke. But then I saw the connection. Of course. This father made his living selling real estate. I could see the advertisement in *The Bluebird Times:* "Beresford Proctor Box for Sale or Rent: exc loc and forage, box vws. Avail immed."

❧

It was impossible to watch the sheep in one field, the bluebirds in another without wondering at how differently these animals raise their young. There were the sheep: animals that give birth to one or two young at a time, young that are able to stand, nurse, and follow their mothers within hours of their birth; young that may never see, but will never need to see, their fathers; young that are fed a nutritious, perfectly formulated sheep drink by their mothers for four to six months before they are weaned. There, in the next field, were the bluebirds: animals that lay four to five small, blue eggs in a nest; eggs that require careful incubation for almost three weeks before their blind, naked contents hatch and begin to demand food on a schedule that pushes both bluebird parents to the limits of their ability to provide.

And there I was watching them, primate and mother of two, fifteen years into raising my children, a task that I share with my husband, a task that will continue until our youngest child is in her twenties, and, if all goes well, our entire lives. We humans parent our young longer than any other animal on earth. For us, parenting is such an essential part of reproduction—such a sine qua non of raising offspring that will survive and make their own way in the world—that we tend to think of parenting as an essential part of *all* reproduction. The bluebirds and the sheep only reinforce this perspective, for though they go about the business of raising their young very differently from the humans who observe or breed them, they are similar in that one parent, at least, spends a great deal of time and effort at the job.

But bluebirds and sheep, like humans, are the exceptions. Parental care, whether it involves the brooding of nestlings inside a nest, the counseling of adolescents on what colleges they might apply to, or the protection and frequent nursing of a young lamb, is not the rule. Most creatures living on the earth today do not bother with such things at all. Beyond producing good-sized eggs and finding, perhaps, a suitable spot to lay them, most animal parents never even see their young. And were they to see them, they would be much more inclined to eat them than to offer them food, protection, or guidance.

These animals, including most fish, frogs, and insects, parent by numbers instead. They play the odds. For reproduction without parental care involves massive overproduction: thousands and thousands of fertilized eggs set afloat in the seas or left to hatch on a leaf or twig. Most, but not all, of these eggs will be eaten. A few will survive. Enough will survive. A female eel, whose job as a mother is over the moment she lays her eggs, lays millions every season. The edible frog *Rana esculenta,* which also limits its parental duties to spawning and fertilization, lays ten thousand.

But what a difference care can make. The Darwin frog of Chile, for which spawning and fertilization are just the first steps in raising young, lays only twenty or thirty eggs each season. After the female has deposited her eggs, the male guards them for several weeks. Then, when the eggs have developed to a certain point, he picks them up with his tongue and presses them into his vocal sac, a deep fold of skin that swells like a balloon when he croaks. There the eggs continue to develop, and there they hatch into tadpoles; there the tadpoles grow and even metamorphose into little frogs. When their tails have fallen off and the froglets are ready to face the world on their own, they leave their father's protection by the same route they entered it—his mouth.

Darwin frogs, bluebirds, sheep, humans are all extreme examples of parental devotion, but even the little things that parents do can make a difference. Before the female salmon lays her eggs at the bottom of a streambed, she excavates a shallow pit—about five to ten inches deep and three to six feet long—with a few strokes of her powerful tail. She deposits her eggs in this pit, then uses her tail to cover them with gravel. Neither she nor her mate shows any interest in the eggs after they are covered, but the shelter of the nest is such that salmon produce far fewer eggs than do fish that drop their eggs in unprotected places.

If the advantages of parental care are so obvious in terms of the number of eggs or young that parents need to produce in order to have young that will survive, then why don't all animals provide it? Why don't they all add it to their reproductive behavior and cut down on the time and energy needed to make all those eggs, most of which are doomed to a very short existence? The answer is that care—parental care—also takes time and energy. A male Darwin frog tending his brood, a female salmon digging her pit, a human father changing his infant's diapers—all these animals are putting time and energy into their young, time and energy that they could be using to look for food themselves or, more to the point, that they could be putting into looking for new mates and making new offspring.

Only in recent decades have scientists understood this: that because all animals have limited resources with which to live and reproduce, natural selection has forced them to "invest" these resources as efficiently as possible. It follows from the laws of thermodynamics. Energy used for one purpose—nursing a young lamb, constructing a nest, nourishing a mouthful of young frogs—cannot be used for another—maintaining one's health, growing, producing more offspring. So the costs of parental care must be weighed against the benefits. And the costs can be measured in reduced parental survival and reproductive success, reductions that have been shown in study after study, animal after animal.

In the Himalayas, wild sheep that are barren or that lose their offspring shortly after birth are more likely to survive periods of extreme weather than are sheep with lambs. Female house martins that raise two broods in one year are much less likely to return the following year than are females that raise only one. In species as diverse as fruit flies, cats, and human beings, sterilized individuals live longer than do those with intact reproductive systems.

Parental care has costs as well as benefits, and animals, as they have evolved, have asked themselves this question: Is it better to have just a few offspring and care for them tenderly or to have many offspring and give each a much shorter shift? Is it better to produce many "cheap" offspring, each of which has a low chance of surviving and finding a mate, or many fewer, expensive offspring, each of which has a higher chance of survival and a higher potential fertility? Is it better to go with quantity or quality?

Over the course of evolution, each species has answered this question differently. Some have opted for quantity, some for quality through a process both simple and deadly. Individuals who gave the wrong answer failed to have offspring that survived. They laid thousands of eggs when a few well-tended eggs would have been better or nursed one offspring for so long that their chance of having additional offspring was greatly reduced.

The result of all this questioning is that each species now has its own pattern of parental care, a pattern of reproduction and parental behavior that distinguishes it as surely as its anatomy or physiology, its plumage or fur color. In all mammals, this pattern includes feeding the young with milk from the mother's mammary glands, but different mammalian species differ greatly in other respects. Rabbit mothers keep their young in well-concealed nests and visit them only every twenty-four hours or so; primate mothers carry theirs about with them. Beaver mothers, human mothers, and wolf mothers raise their young with the help of their mates, but most mammalian mothers parent alone.

Many of us are used to thinking of our bodies—our eyes, our brains, our limbs, our internal organs—as being shaped by evolution, but not our behavior, especially our behavior during the intensely personal experiences of birth and parenting. The idea feels slightly uncomfortable, like a pair of pants with a waist that is too tight, a wool sweater on an unexpected warm day. Yet how could these behaviors—the Darwin frog pressing eggs into his vocal sac, the salmon excavating her pit, the human mother cradling her infant—have come about except by gradual changes subjected, at each and every step of the way, to the ruthless scrutiny of natural selection until just the right compromise between costs and benefits, parent and offspring survival was reached? Animals didn't think through their options in deciding how to behave. Natural selection did the thinking for them. Individuals with one particular set of behaviors wound up with more copies of their genes in subsequent generations; individuals without those behaviors, with less.

But when would an animal begin to care for its young? When would it be advantageous to add parental care to the act of reproduction? To trade quantity for quality? To take the risks that caring for one's offspring entails? No one can say exactly how parental care

in any one species came about or why it took one form and not another (what small random changes in behavior or egg production
were seized upon by natural selection and why), but in recent years
researchers have come to appreciate the kinds of environments in
which parental care is likely to evolve.

On the one hand, parental care often results when animals adapt
to stable, predictable environments—environments in which animals
tend to live longer, grow larger, and reproduce at intervals instead of
all at once. In the structured environment of a coral reef, for example, where fish tend to occupy home ranges or territories and to return to certain places for feeding and shelter, they are much more
likely to practice some form of parental care than in the open ocean.

But parental care can also evolve when a species is threatened by
predators or when it expands into an entirely new, possibly stressful
environment. Then, parents might need to do something new for
their young in order to advance them to the stage where they are able
to survive on their own. *Bledius spectabilis* is a beetle that lives in
mudflats on the coast of Northern Europe, and were it not for the
mother beetle's constant digging that keeps her burrow well venti-
lated, her brood would be suffocated by the incoming tides. Crickets
that nest in deep soil and feed their young on moist vegetable matter
have had to become experts in fungus control. We tend to think of
parental care only in terms of protection, feeding, guidance, and comfort, because those are the things we do for our own children, but for
other animals, aeration and fungus control are much more important.

Researchers have also found that parental care is common among
animals that depend on rich but distant or scattered food sources,
schools of fish, for instance, or carrion or prey. Crowned eagles often
search thousands of square miles to find prey. Because their food is
so difficult to come by, these birds raise only a single offspring at a
time, and they take seventeen months to do it. Seventeen months of
searching for food and bringing it back to the nest before a young
crowned eagle is ready to go off on its own. Burying beetles (also

known as gravedigger or undertaker beetles) feed on small dead animals and are also devoted parents. After locating the corpse of a mouse or bird, both male and female beetle shape it into a ball and dig a burrow in which they seal themselves and their prize. The female lays her eggs in a well on top of the ball, and, when the young hatch, they feed on the rotting flesh of the corpse as well as beg for food from their parents. Their parents respond by squirting a dark liquid from their mouths into the mouths of their young. The parents' job is not limited to feeding the young. They must also keep the carcass free from fungi by carefully clipping it with their mandibles and free from bacteria by coating it with a special antibacterial secretion produced in their abdomens.

So animals provide parental care in different kinds of environments. And while the care they give to their young is wonderfully diverse—even among some closely related species—they do tend to be constrained by the kind of animal they are: warm-blooded or cold-blooded, vertebrate or invertebrate, mammal or bird. To understand why animals parent the way they do and why parental care is more common among some groups of animals than among others, one must first understand some of these constraints.

Parental care is fairly rare among the invertebrates—animals like insects and worms that lack an internal skeleton—for two reasons. First of all, invertebrates are cold-blooded. Because their internal temperature approximates that of the environment, they are unable to incubate their eggs—to raise the temperature of the eggs above the ambient temperature—thus eliminating the most important reason why warm-blooded animals stay with their eggs. Second, most invertebrates are constrained in their parental care by their size. Because invertebrates are fairly small animals, they are unable to defend their young against predators.

Burying beetles and *Bledius spectabilis* are two exceptional parents in this group. But there are others: wood roaches dig and defend a long-lasting, stable burrow system under rotting logs and take an astonishing three to five years to raise a single brood; the social insects—bees, wasps, ants, and termites living in large colonies—have highly organized methods of brooding, feeding, and protecting their offspring. By and large, though, in invertebrates, natural selection has tended to favor the alternative strategy: production of large numbers of eggs.

Even though many vertebrates are cold-blooded and cannot incubate their eggs, parental care is more common among vertebrates because an internal skeleton supports a much larger body, and a larger body means more defense capability.

Nowhere is this advantage more apparent than in the parental behavior of freshwater fish. Fish cannot incubate their eggs, but because of the size factor (fish fry are very much smaller than adult fish, and predators are usually about the same size as adults), fish *are* able to guard their eggs and their fry and, sometimes, to transport them from one place to another.

Only about 16 percent of all fish species actually care for their offspring after egg laying, but more than half of all freshwater species do. This is no coincidence. In the open ocean, where water conditions are somewhat constant and egg predators somewhat spread out, free-floating eggs have a reasonable chance of survival. But in freshwater, conditions tend to be extremely variable and eggs are much more likely to be preyed upon.

Certainly the most famous fish parents are the freshwater three-spined stickleback and the sea horse, a sea-dwelling relative of the stickleback that lives in very shallow, inshore waters, where it is buffeted by storms and winds and encounters many predators—fish, crabs, skates, rays, and human collectors.

The male stickleback begins his paternal duties by building a nest out of weeds, which he cements together with a material secreted from his kidney. After enticing a female to lay her eggs in the nest, he fertilizes the eggs, then guards them and later the fry, charging at predators and tirelessly retrieving fry in his mouth. The male sea horse shows an even greater devotion to his young by incubating his mate's eggs within his body, by actually becoming pregnant. The female deposits her eggs in a special brood pouch on the male's tail, and the male then fertilizes them and seals the pouch. For several weeks he protects, aerates, and nourishes the developing young, finally releasing them as tiny, independent sea horses.

Protection of the young may be common among freshwater fish, but feeding of the young is rare because here size is a disadvantage. Adult fish are so much larger than their fry that they feed on very different foods. The discus fish of the Amazon Basin is one of the few fish that has evolved a solution to this problem. In this species, both male and female secrete from the sides of their bodies a nutritious mucus, which their fry graze on. Fry feed on only one parent at a time, and a changing of the guard occurs when the absent parent returns and the current sitter spurts off at a speed too fast for the fry to follow.

Like fish, most reptiles cannot incubate their eggs, and most do not exhibit parental care. The exceptions are crocodiles, caimans, and alligators, all of which have come up with ways of increasing the temperature of their eggs and all of which are large enough to ward off predators. The females of all these animals lay their eggs in large nests, which they cover with mud and/or vegetation and defend against intruders. When American alligators are about to hatch, they call from inside their shells, prompting their mother to start tearing the hard, sun-baked material off the top. Many crocodilians stay with their young for days and even weeks after they have hatched, protecting them and leading them to the water to feed. If attacked, the young give high-pitched distress calls, which signal the mother to charge.

Some snakes also make solicitous mothers but usually only those that are large enough (the python) or venomous enough (the African and Asian cobras) to defend their eggs effectively against predators. The python female coils tightly around her eggs so that they are completely hidden. In doing so, she both defends them and warms them by a method unique to pythons: shivering thermogenesis. Through rhythmic muscular contractions of her body, the female python produces enough heat to keep the egg mass at a relatively high and constant temperature. Energetically, shivering thermogenesis is an extremely costly method of incubation, but by quickening development of the eggs, it has allowed the python to penetrate new and colder environments. Some snakes have also been observed to help their young hatch, but no good evidence has been found for the often-repeated stories that snakes swallow their young to protect them or that they nourish their young inside their stomachs. Nor, sadly enough, is there anything to the tale that rattlesnakes croon to their offspring by softly rattling.

Certain vertebrates have a definite logistical problem when it comes to child care. These are the amphibians—frogs, newts, and toads. It is a problem hinted at in their name—*amphi*=both, *bios*=life. Adult amphibians spend their life on land, but young amphibians live in the water, making close association between parent and offspring something of a dilemma. Most amphibians lay their eggs on or near the water and have nothing more to do with them, but a few species—the Darwin frog included—have found a way around this conflict in lifestyles.

The male midwife toad carries strings of eggs around his legs, moistening them with water as needed and later releasing the hatched tadpoles into water. The female of the extraordinary Australian frog *Rheobatrachus silus* swallows her eggs after they are laid and fertilized, then gives birth to froglets several weeks later. Because the eggs develop inside her stomach, the female must stop all gastric activity— all digestion and all eating—during her pseudopregnancy lest she digest the eggs she is incubating. When she finally does give birth, it is by projectile vomiting.

Dart-poison frogs of Central America lay their eggs on land, guard them, then transport the hatched tadpoles on their backs to streams or tiny pools of water that collect in air plants. In a few of these frogs, named for the practice of some Central and South American Indians of extracting a poison from the frogs' skin and using it to coat the tips of their darts, the females also visit the tadpoles regularly, bringing them eggs to eat that have not been fertilized.

Which brings us back to birds—egg layers like most other animals but warm-blooded. The eggs of birds, unlike those of cold-blooded animals, must be kept within a narrow temperature range; otherwise they will freeze—or roast—and the embryos inside will fail to develop normally. Among the thousands of bird species in existence today, all but a very few rely on parental care, incubation after egg laying, to accomplish this. The exceptions are the brood parasites, birds like the European cuckoo and the American cowbird, which lay their eggs in the nests of other birds and depend, therefore, on the kindness of strangers, the parental care of others.

Few birds, though, end their care with incubation. Most also care for their young after they have hatched by brooding them or feeding them, protecting them or keeping their nest clean, teaching them to forage for food or to sing the song of their species. The exceptions are again the brood parasites and the megapodes, large-footed birds of Australia and southeastern Asia that perform a yeoman's job during incubation (these birds build huge piles of dirt and rotting vegetation in which they lay and incubate their eggs) but have given up every other trace of parental care.

When the megapode chick hatches, it must dig itself out of its pile and face the world entirely on its own. It doesn't ever see its parents, but, then again, it is so well developed—fully feathered, fully sighted, with strong feet and fully developed muscular and sensory systems— that it doesn't need to. A chick like the eastern bluebird, on the other hand, hatches naked and blind and requires parents to feed it, protect it, remove its fecal sacs, and keep it warm for three weeks before it is even ready to leave its nest. Once outside the nest, it continues to rely on its parents for another two weeks or so for food and for education in such matters as the correct way to dismember a grasshopper.

Megapodes have the most precocial, or well developed, chicks of any bird species; the eastern bluebird some of the most altricial, or least developed. The word *altricial* (pronounced to rhyme with the last two syllables of *superficial*) comes from the Latin word for "feeder," though food is just one of the many things that the parents of altricial chicks provide for their young. "Needer" would be a better description of these creatures that hatch with their eyes sealed shut and with featherless, translucent bellies.

Megapodes and bluebirds represent two extremes in avian reproductive strategy, but every possible intermediate is known, and species are now classified as superprecocial, precocial, subprecocial, semialtricial, and altricial. In general, birds that have precocial chicks lay large numbers of large eggs, which have a high yolk or energy content and hatch into well-developed, well-feathered chicks that leave the nest shortly after hatching but may require their parents for brooding (especially at night), protection, guidance, and some feeding. Altricial birds, on the other hand, produce smaller clutches of smaller eggs, which hatch into less-developed chicks that always require a lengthy period of brooding, feeding, and protection.

Overall, 80 percent of bird species are altricial, but at different latitudes, different strategies are favored. In cool climates, the precocial chick's ability to keep itself warm is a great advantage. In warm climates, altricial chicks may be less expensive to rear because they require less brooding. In the tropics, where birds face many predators, there may also be an advantage to the altricial strategy because of the smaller altricial clutch size. A bird that loses a small clutch suffers less of an energetic loss than does a bird that loses a large one.

Mammals are also warm-blooded animals, but unlike birds most incubate their eggs internally, in the uterus, and give birth to live young. The egg-laying platypus and the spiny anteater are the only exceptions. In addition, all mammals have feeding of the young built into their reproductive strategy. They all have mammary glands with which they nourish their young. So they all are committed to a period of parental care after birth. During evolution, this form of care was so advantageous to the survival of mammalian young that it became fixed as mammals developed into the diverse animals we know and are today.

Lactation may be the defining feature of mammals, but parental care in most mammals neither begins nor ends with this activity. It begins with retention of the fertilized egg in the uterus and ends for some long after weaning. Besides suckling, it can include building nests or excavating burrows; keeping the young warm, safe, and clean and providing them with foods other than milk; carrying them and instructing them in the ways of hunting and foraging and appropriate social conduct; and giving comfort and emotional support. Because it is the female mammal who gestates and lactates, she is usually the primary caregiver, but in some mammals individuals other than the mother—fathers or close kin—provide care that substitutes for that of the mother or that translates into milk for the mother: active defense of a territory to exclude competitors for food, for example, or actual food, as in the regurgitated offerings of male wolves and hunting dogs.

Like birds, mammals also have twin reproductive strategies and bear young that are either precocial or altricial. But in mammals, a species's choice of strategy often has to do with whether it is predator or prey. Predators—animals that are capable of protecting themselves and their young—can afford to give birth to helpless, sightless young, which they keep warm and protected within the confines of a nest or den while those young continue to develop. Animals that live with the distinct possibility of winding up as someone else's dinner, on the other hand, need their young well formed at birth. Those young must be able to stand, walk, hear, see, keep warm, and run for cover in a very short period of time.

Almost all carnivorous species have altricial young; almost all grazing (or ungulate) species—my sheep, for example—have precocial young.[1] Primates, including humans, share features of both patterns. Generally, their young are quite helpless at birth. They cannot walk or move around by themselves, yet most are born with fur and are capable of seeing, hearing, and clinging to their mothers. This mixed strategy reflects not so much the primate's place as predator or prey (most primates are predominantly vegetarian and are only occasional prey for other animals) as their adaptation to life in the treetops. Primate infants are called secondarily altricial because their altriciality or immaturity was superimposed on a precocial background as this adaptation took place. In the treetops, precocial infants cannot follow their mothers at birth, nor can they be safely left behind in nests. So as primates moved into the trees for protection and access to food, mothers had to evolve new ways of caring for their infants, and infants had to evolve new ways of staying with their mothers. And in the treetops, flexible learned behaviors—as opposed to behaviors that are more instinctive or innate—played an increasingly important part in survival.

For flexibility—and brainpower—are the real trade-offs in these twin strategies of mammals and birds. A dim light that turns on quickly versus a powerful spotlight that is slow to warm up. In precocial animals, the brain is more fully developed at birth or hatching. Pathways are set; behavior patterns are already formed. Learning, the only means by which the experience of one individual can be transmitted to a new generation, does not play as much of a role in their lives. The brains of altricial young, on the other hand, finish developing in the rich experiential context of the real world (rather than the dull, predictable context of the uterus or egg). There, they are truly shaped by experience and by learning, and there the behaviors of these animals are fine-tuned to ever-changing environments and ever-new sources of danger.

Homo sapiens' distant ancestors embarked upon this flexible, high-brainpower, altricial strategy when they were living in trees, and hominids continued it as they descended from trees and adapted to life on the ground, taking it to greater and greater extremes. At birth, the brain of a chimpanzee, our nearest living relative, is one half its full adult size, but the brain of a human infant is just one quarter. Three quarters of the human brain's development takes place in the real world, an adaptation that has given humans the ability to move into and inhabit every part of the globe and one that has demanded extraordinary amounts of parental care.

While the chimpanzee is dependent on its mother for six years (as its brain develops and it grows to close to its full adult size), the human child, even the child of hunter-gatherers, is dependent on its parents for close to two decades. Our species has truly traded quantity for quality. That has been our reproductive bargain, our way of ensuring that our young survive.

❧

May was a very busy time for the mammals and birds at my latitude in southern New York. The sheep had all had their lambs, and the trees and bushes were full of mockingbirds, bluebirds, blue jays, chickadees, and house finches.

I had never seen so many house finches. No sooner did I put out a basket of hanging geraniums or a pot of begonias than these small, raspberry-streaked birds began to investigate it as a possible nesting site. There were house finches in the pots and house finches behind many of the shutters. One day there were four pale blue finch eggs lying nestless in one of the geraniums, and I wondered at the mishap that had resulted in such a non sequitur.

Yet I wasn't entirely surprised by the finches' numbers; over the winter I had noticed that a group of these birds had found a very clever spot in which to ride out the snowstorms of that year. This was the top of the clothes dryer vent, behind a first-story shutter. All winter long, any time any of us would open the kitchen door, finches would swoop from behind the shutter, singing their lusty, melodious song, just about as cheerful on a cold day as a cup of hot cider. In early spring, I took a look at their accommodations and found a winter nest thickly padded with sheep's wool and at least six inches deep. When I looked a few weeks later, a small, fine grass nest sat on top of the thick wool base.

Then, toward the end of May, I began to miss the song of finches and looked in the nest on top of the vent to see if anything had happened. In this elaborate, multitiered construction of grass and wool, situated to receive thousands of extra BTUs of heat a week (BTUs which would spare the parents much incubation time) were four pale blue eggs—all broken. Animals other than myself, it was obvious, had been watching the comings and goings of these innovative avians. I don't know what actually happened to the adult finches—whether one was taken as it incubated its eggs or whether the nest was abandoned after the eggs were plundered—but the plundering turned what had been a finch success story into a much more familiar tale of boom and bust.

The bluebirds in the Vermont box were easier to follow—and more successful. On May 10, the day our sheep were being shorn, the bluebirds hatched. I went down to the box between ewes and was startled to see brown instead of the blue of the eggs. My first, foolish thought was that the eggs had been taken . . . then the brown mass at the bottom of the nest shifted a little. The nestlings were mostly stomach, and their eyes were sealed shut. They would remain that way for five or six days, about the amount of time it would take for their first feathers to appear. I picked one of the nestlings up (birds cannot smell, so they do not, as some believe, reject their young after they've been handled); it was very light and unexpectedly warm, like holding a cupcake with a lit candle in it, as a friend once described it.

When I stepped back from the box, the male bluebird swooped in with something that looked like a small spider. Before the nestlings leave the nest, in three weeks, each will have received about two thousand such feedings, half from each parent. Both male and female will have flown over three hundred miles to satisfy the appetites of their young. Their feathers "will be tattered and soiled with excrement," as one ornithologist has written, and "countless intruders and potential predators will have been driven off." For *Sialia sialis,* the eastern bluebird, that is just what it means to be a parent.

III

Father Wolf, Mother Bear— Who Cares?

Fathers, Margaret Mead once observed, are a biological ne- cessity but a social accident. She was referring to hu- mans, but for my sheep, for the five or six black-faced Hampshire ewes that we breed most years, this is truly the case. The only time that these females see a male of their species, other than their own male offspring, is dur- ing six weeks in the fall when we rent a ram from Jeff Traver, a breeder of purebred Hampshires.

Our most recent ram had been a promising show animal before he developed the habit of scratching his itchy head and neck on fence posts, trees, or whatever else he could find. When the wool around his neck turned black and patchy, Jeff had to give up showing him and the ram began a second career as a stud. He came to us directly from a prior job: inseminating two Southdown ewes that had never been able to get pregnant because, I was told, they were too fat. It wasn't that they were overfed, simply that this breed of sheep is very efficient at turning sparse pasture into meat. They can get fat on air, Jeff says.

Despite his threadbare neck, this ram was a handsome creature, with fine, sloping shoulders and a long, black face—not at all like some of our rent-a-rams. The worst, a thick, lumpy-faced beast with mottled wool and the utterly unlikely name of Oh to Be, looked like an ovine version of Moby Dick; yet he was so well endowed—so totally overqualified for the job of inseminating our few ewes—that I found myself blushing as Jeff brought him off the truck. Like all the rams, he did his job well, but the lambs he sired grew up into unappealing, lumpy-faced rams and ewes, all deserving of the name we gave to the ewe that resembled her father the most: Woe to Be, short for Woe to Be the Daughter of Oh to Be.

Our handsome ram with the patchy neck didn't have a name—just a number. When he finished with our ewes, Jeff took him to the slaughterhouse. That's the way it is sometimes for a biological necessity but a social accident. Even in the wild, rams only associate with ewes during rutting. When male lambs are weaned by their mothers, they go off to join all-male gangs while female lambs stay with the flock. One of the distinctive features of sheep and most other grazing animals is the rarity of long-term male-female bonds, the absence of any paternal feeling.

The male bluebird, on the other hand, is a distinctly different subject. Besides locating a nesting site, staking out a territory, and guarding the female as she builds her nest and incubates her eggs, the male bluebird contributes directly to the growth and survival of his off-spring with a thousand or so offerings of spiders and caterpillars for each nestling.

Nor is the male dispensable in species of freshwater fish where the male guards the fry or in sea horses, where the male is actually impregnated with his mate's eggs. Bluebirds, sheep, fish, all raise the question of why the female cares for the young in some species and the male, or the male and female together, in others. But the pregnant male sea horse also raises an even more fundamental question. What does it mean to be a male . . . or a female?

How do we know that the pregnant sea horse is a male? Why not call it a female? From our mammalian perspective, in which only females become pregnant and only males can walk away from the consequences of sex, this is an entirely reasonable question, and the answer is surprisingly simple.

In all species that practice sexual reproduction (and that includes almost all life-forms, almost all animals and plants) there are two types of individuals. One type—the female—produces a small number of large sex cells or eggs; the other type—the male—produces a much larger number of small sex cells or sperm. We know it is the male sea horse that incubates the eggs because he produces the smaller sex cells.

In cold-blooded animals and in birds, the difference in the size of sperm and eggs is particularly pronounced (a rooster's sperm is microscopic, but a hen's egg is big enough and nutritious enough to feed a developing embryo for several weeks). But even in mammals, the female's egg is many times larger than the male's sperm. In all animals, the disparity is great enough to explain many of the differences between the sexes. For instance:

- Because females produce their larger, more nutritious, more expensive eggs at a slower rate than males produce their smaller, less expensive sperm, females have little to gain from mating with a large number of males. A mammalian female might produce just one or two eggs each estrous cycle and might need to incubate her fertilized egg or eggs for months; a mammalian male produces millions of sperm every day. Males can gain from as many matings as they can muster and tend toward philandering and promiscuity; females tend toward coyness and a greater selectivity.

- Because females produce the larger sex cells, they have more invested in those cells than males have in their sperm. They are, at the moment of fertilization, more committed to the fertilized egg than are their mates. And because they are more committed at this moment, they are more likely to continue to be committed. They are the ones most likely to care for their offspring, the ones less likely to desert and look for new mating opportunities. If they do desert, it will always cost them more than it would their mates— more time and more energy—to raise new offspring to the same point of development.

Every sexually reproducing animal feels the effects of these unequal sex cells to some extent. In mammals, one small step in maternal commitment has led to another, and the female now incubates the fertilized egg inside her uterus, the female produces milk to nourish the infant, the female usually provides all the warmth, protection, emotional support, and education required by her young. In humans, a copulation costing a male almost nothing may trigger a nine-month investment by a female followed by years and years of care in which the male may or may not participate.

"No wonder," sighed a friend of mine when I told her about this fundamental difference between males and females, this cast of the sexual die. She had just missed several days of work to stay home with children who had the flu, and so she had been pondering the inequities of care. She considers herself a well-educated, well-informed person and couldn't believe, she said, that she had not looked at the fundamentals of the situation this way before.

Yet the size of sex cells cannot be all there is to mating and parenting . . . to male and female behavior. If it was, why would the male sea horse incubate his mate's large eggs? Why would most human males choose to stick around and support their families (even if they're not usually the ones to stay home with a sick child)? Biologists did not have good answers to these questions until the early 1970s, when Robert Trivers, an excitable and extremely brilliant graduate student at Harvard, turned his attention from mathematics toward issues of parental care. In five spectacular years, this innovative thinker, who suffered from manic-depressive syndrome, came up with explanations for some of the most puzzling aspects of animal behavior, including the vast differences in how males interact with their young. As Edward O. Wilson, one of Trivers's advisers at Harvard, described him, "When he was up, he was dazzling; when he was down, he was terrifying."

Because of the disparity in the size of their sex cells, males and females have adopted very different reproductive strategies, Trivers argued in "Parental Investment and Sexual Selection," one in a series of groundbreaking papers. The tendency of males may be toward promiscuity, but because females invest more initially, they are in the position to be choosy and, by carefully selecting their mates, to shape male behavior. If a female only mates with a male that brings her food or that gathers sticks with which she can build her nest, for example, and the female raises more offspring than do females that mate with just any male, then pretty soon only those males that share food or offer building materials will get to mate. And pretty soon food sharing or help in nest construction will be part of the male makeup.

Generally, as Trivers pointed out, female choosiness has taken one of two directions: either the females of a species select mates on the basis of their strength and virility, mates that will give them the biggest, most vigorous offspring, or they select mates on the basis of their willingness to care for those offspring.

The first strategy, the he-man approach, as it has been dubbed by Richard Dawkins, the author of *The Selfish Gene,* is evidenced by sheep, as well as lions, walrus, and numerous other polygamous, harem-forming animals. The second strategy, that of female bluebirds and sea horses, Dawkins called the domestic bliss approach, since it often leads to monogamous (or somewhat monogamous) relationships. Where he-man strategies are the rule, males are usually larger and more colorful than their mates. Where both males and females care for their young, the sexes are much closer in size and coloration. In species in which males provide more care than do their mates, females tend to be bigger and brighter, for it is they who compete for males, and for their willingness to tend the young.

Trivers was one of the first to understand this. "What governs the operation of sexual selection [competition of one sex for members of the opposite sex]," he wrote, "is the relative parental investment of the sexes in their offspring."

Clothes may or may not make the man, but paternal affection, it seems, certainly does. Male cardinals, with their brilliant red plumage, are far too eye-catching to be parents that visit the nest regularly. In humans, males are only somewhat bigger than females, indicating that our pattern of parental care, which has been shaped by thousands of years of natural selection, is imbalanced but not terribly so. The sexual dimorphism of human males is nothing like the male peacock's trailing tail, or the male gray seal's extra three hundred pounds.

But how do females decide which strategy to adopt? They don't, of course. Natural selection decides for them, in its usual cutthroat game of winner take all. Females that choose males on the basis of their being able to beat all other males in jousting and horn-locking contests when what they really need are males that will protect them or provide food for their offspring fail to have offspring that survive and fail, therefore, to leave their behavioral tendencies—their preference for strong, aggressive mates—in the gene pool. Females that make the right choice, select the right door given the needs of their young in the environment in which they are being raised, have offspring that survive and reproduce.

Paternal care is not completely up to the female, though, as Trivers also pointed out. Male responses to female selection also vary, depending on several factors: the amount of care the male is able to provide, for example, and the possibility of additional matings. In general, the sex with the greater ability to provide care is the one that is selected to do so, and, in general, males do not take on parental care if caring interferes greatly with additional matings. In the shallow, turbulent waters of the Atlantic coast, where tiny sea horses hang on by their tails to stalks of seaweed or the roots of a mangrove, these territorial, fairly immobile fish rarely encounter others of their kind. Males do not have that many opportunities to mate, so they may not be giving up all that much when they settle down to incubate their mates' eggs.

But the most important factor in how males respond to female selection is the male's confidence that the offspring he will be caring for are his. Biologists call this his confidence of paternity or paternal certainty, and they have found that only those males that have a reasonable amount of it (because of the environment or the social setting in which they live or because of some behavior they have adopted) have developed male care.

"It is a wise father that knows his own child," says Launcelot in *The Merchant of Venice*. Males that provide care for their young go to great lengths to ensure that they are, in fact, the fathers. Mate guarding, copulatory plugs, chastity belts, infanticide, chemical abortifacients are just some of the animal world's many anticuckold devices. When a new male takes over a troop of langurs, long-tailed monkeys that live in the rain forests of Asia, he kills all the infants in the troop. This act, seemingly one of wanton cruelty and aggression, frees him from caring for unrelated infants. It also means that the mothers of those infants will be ready to mate with him much sooner than if he had allowed them to finish nursing their young to the point of nutritional independence. It is not that male animals dream up these behaviors in order to protect themselves; rather, those males that lacked them, those that cared for just any offspring, were the losers. Their own genes failed to survive.

Not all the females in any one species need adopt the same strategy; not all the males need respond in the same way. Most human societies are monogamous, but the human species is classified by biologists as moderately polygamous because there are cultures in which it is fairly common for men to have more than one wife. Males could not express this, their underlying tendency toward promiscuity, if females always denied them the opportunity, if all females stuck to a strictly monogamous strategy. In some places it is preferable, apparently, to be the second wife of a high-status man with many resources than the only wife of a lower-status individual.

Similarly, some birds long thought to be monogamous, the eastern bluebird for one, are now known to have a low but significant number of liaisons on the side, extrapair copulations as they are called. The usual explanation for these outside liaisons is that they benefit both males and females: males, for obvious reasons, and females, because they allow those that are mated to disappointing males to garner superior genes for their progeny while keeping the lesser males around to help raise the brood. But an alternative, divorce-remarriage explanation has recently been proposed by Judith Stamps of the University of California at Davis. Stamps argues that a female might mate with a desirable, though already-mated male not just for sperm but because the male has a better home territory. Should this well-situated male lose his current mate, he might be more likely to select the upwardly mobile female as a replacement because of their previous tryst, and she would benefit from both his genes and his real estate. "There's more to copulation than a transfer of sperm," Stamps observes. "These females may be thinking of their futures."[1]

It is not so much, then, that females are coy monogamists and males helpless profligates as the sexes used to be characterized, but that each sex, each individual, is working to strike his or her best reproductive bargain.

For all animals, the goal is to produce as many offspring as possible in their time on earth. (This sounds shocking, deliberately contentious, but it is, if you think about it, only the logical extension of

Darwin's ideas, the inevitable outcome of a world run by natural selection. And it is not the goal of animals in any conscious way. Rather,
only those animals that behaved as if this were their goal had offspring
enough so that their genes—and behavioral tendencies—have survived.) For some animals the best way to produce offspring is to care
for them during certain stages of their development. But care gets in
the way of producing more offspring unless, of course, you can get
your mate to do the caring while you continue to sow new seeds or
incubate new eggs. This is the endgame that all sexually reproducing parents play. Males, because of their small, inexpensive sex cells,
just happen to be better at it than females.

Nowhere is the game more clearly laid out than in the British ornithologist Nicholas Davies's fascinating study of the dunnock, a
small, English, sparrowlike bird. Like bluebirds, dunnocks had been
thought to be monogamous, but when Davies looked closely at their
reproductive behavior, he found much promiscuity instead—by both
males and females. Dunnocks are capable of forming a bizarre array
of domestic arrangements. In just the small group of dunnocks living in the Cambridge University Botanic Garden, where Davies con-
ducted his study, he found ménages à deux, trois, quatre, and cinq.
In one part of the garden, a pair of dunnocks was living a quiet,
monogamous life while next door a female was mated with two males.
In neighboring territories, one male was mated with two females and
three females with two males.

What could the dunnocks be up to? In order to find out, Davies
banded the birds and their chicks, then used DNA analysis or "fingerprinting" to determine the parentage of the chicks and the reproductive success of the adults. Female dunnocks, he discovered, left the
most progeny when one female was paired to two males and her
nestlings fed by two fathers. They fared less well in monogamous relationships and worse still in arrangements in which two females
shared the attentions of one male. Males, on the other hand, fared best
when they were paired with more than one female, less well in

monogamous arrangements, and worst of all in nests where they had to share the affections of their mate with another male.

The arrangement that made the best reproductive sense for females, in other words, was just the opposite of the one that made the best reproductive success for males. And in the bucolic splendor of the botanic garden, each sex competed to force upon the other the type of relationship that suited him or her best—driving off members of the same sex when possible, enticing new partners with sexual advances. The female won when she could defend against all other females a territory that was too large to be defended, in turn, by a single male. The male won when he could defend two female territories against the intrusions of all other males. For both sexes, monogamy was a stalemate, an arrangement in which neither female nor male was able to gain a second mate.

So much for cooperation between the sexes, for devoted pairs working together to raise their young. Reproduction and parenting used to be thought of as collaborative ventures, but biologists now recognize the conflict inherent in sex. "Every marriage is a battle between two families struggling to reproduce themselves," a noted family therapist has observed. Mother and father are interested in different genetic halves of the same offspring. There may be advantages for both in cooperating to rear those offspring, but each may do even better by forcing the other parent to invest more while he or she pursues new mating opportunities.

Nor do animals stop with exploiting their mates. Males exploit the care of other males (the reason why paternal certainty is such a big issue); brood parasites like the cuckoo exploit the parental care of other species; and females, as biologists have been finding out, exploit the care of other females. Even, or perhaps I should say especially, bluebird females.

Several years ago, before the technology of DNA analysis was available, Patricia Gowaty, an evolutionary biologist at the University of Georgia, used blood protein analysis to determine the relationships of nestlings and adults at twenty-seven bluebird boxes in northwest South Carolina. She expected that a certain percentage of the nestlings at any box would be unrelated to the adult male that was feeding them because she knew that some eastern bluebirds engage in extrapair liaisons or matings on the side. But Gowaty did not expect to find nestlings unrelated to the female that was feeding them. In some of her boxes, females were taking care of nestlings hatched from eggs that could not possibly have been laid by them, eggs that could only have been laid or deposited in the nest by another bluebird.

In Gowaty's study, one quarter of the nestlings were unrelated to at least one of their parents. Between egg dumping and extrapair copulations, one out of every four nestlings was receiving parental care from at least one unrelated adult. But the problem was far greater for bluebird mothers than for fathers. Five percent of the adult males were caring for an unrelated nestling as compared with 15 percent of the adult females (a result which could only mean that the female that dumped an egg in another female's nest had often mated with that female's mate).

Though her results came as a surprise to Gowaty, they made sense of the fierce battles she had observed between female bluebirds, battles that were most intense at egg-laying time. "I have seen female bluebirds maim and even kill each other, outcomes I have never witnessed in fights between males," noted Gowaty. She now sees these battles as a logical countermeasure to egg dumping, a behavior that protects females from bestowing costly parental care on unrelated nestlings and that is the equivalent of mate guarding in males. For bluebirds, at least, maternal certainty is just as much an issue as paternal certainty, and bluebird females are even more likely than males to exploit each other's care.[2]

Now that all these conflicts—between males and females, males and males, females and females, and species and species—as well as the conditions under which males care for their young are on the table, we can look at how they play out in different animals. Only now can we begin to understand why the male wolf might bring back meat to the den where his mate nurses their litter of pups. Or why the ewe parents alone. Why most human fathers support their children throughout their lifetimes, even making provisions for them after their deaths. For Margaret Mead was wrong when she said that fathers, human fathers, are biological necessities but social accidents. Like many before and after her, she was not fully aware that animal fathers can contribute to the survival and upbringing of their offspring in a variety of ways. Human fathers have rarely been responsible for the day-to-day care of their children, but, in other ways, they have been essential in their survival.

But first, let's look at the cold-blooded fathers, like fish.

Sea horses, as it turns out, are the rule rather than the exception when it comes to fish, gender, and parental care. In those species of fish that care for their young after egg laying, fathers usually do all the caring. This seems strange until you consider the paternal certainty of fish. When fish mate, fertilization occurs outside the female's body. This external fertilization, as it is called, requires so much synchronization in the mating behavior of males and females that males can usually be sure they are not attempting to fertilize, and care for, eggs that have already been fertilized by another.

The male sand goby that lives in the waters off the coast of France searches for an empty cockleshell with which to begin his nest. He turns the shell over so the concave side is facing down, then excavates the sand from underneath. Next, he heaps sand on top, leaving only a narrow channel for access. When his nest is ready, he escorts a female to it, then waits outside while she slips in and deposits her eggs. When she leaves he fertilizes the eggs, then guards them until the fry hatch, confident that no sperm other than his could have done the job. The male sea horse takes this process one step further. Because he fertilizes his mate's eggs within his pouch, he is 100 percent certain that they have been fertilized by his sperm, 100 percent certain that the care he gives those eggs will benefit his genes alone.

Paternal certainty is a precondition of male care, but it is not by itself an explanation of male care, and the prevalence of male guarding in fish was a puzzle to biologists until Richard Dawkins proposed a plausible solution in *The Selfish Gene*. Because fish eggs are shed before fish sperm, Dawkins suggested, males are the partners last in possession of the fertilized eggs. They are the partners left holding the bag, so to speak, and the decision is theirs whether to tend those eggs or abandon them to their fate. If those males that hung around their eggs—if only to feed, perhaps, and if only for a short time—left more progeny than those that did not, paternal care might slowly evolve.

Fish inhabit a medium in which eggs and sperm, after they've been released from the body, do not dry up. So fish can practice external fertilization. Land-dwelling animals, by contrast, must fertilize their eggs internally, and with internal fertilization female care predominates. Not only is the male less certain that his is the sperm that fertilized the female's eggs but male and female are likely to have separated before the female actually lays her eggs. So now it is the female left holding the bag, or the baby.

Salamanders are a good example of the intimate connection between how eggs are fertilized and who cares for them. There are five species of salamanders, or tailed amphibians, that fertilize their eggs externally and exhibit some degree of parental care, and in all five the males do the caring. There are twelve species with internal fertilization and parental care, and in all twelve the females do the work.

All warm-blooded animals must provide care to their temperature-sensitive young. And all warm-blooded animals, birds and mammals, also practice internal fertilization. It's easy enough to explain, therefore, why mammals are so strongly biased toward female care but not so easy to explain why in birds care by both parents is the norm. Males provide direct child care in less than 5 percent of mammalian species,[3] but in over 90 percent of bird species both male and female tend to their young.

Reduced maternal certainty in birds may have something to do with this (the avian female's ever-present worry that the egg she is incubating is not an egg she has laid), but a number of other factors certainly do as well. Most important, in most bird species both sexes are, in theory, equally capable of doing all the postegg-laying chores. Neither sex has a built-in advantage as far as caregiving goes. In mammals, by contrast, the female comes with a uterus for incubating the fertilized egg and with mammary glands for feeding the young. Most males can do little beyond providing protection for the young.

Another factor is the sparse nature of most avian food supplies. The food of birds, compared with that of most animals, is widely scattered. A few dogwood berries here, a few mulberries there. By necessity, most birds are long-distance foragers; young birds *need* the attentions of both parents to be well nourished. It's not surprising that the majority of bird species in which the male provides little care—ducks, for example—are fed little if at all by their parents. These species also tend to live in grasslands or marshes, where food is concentrated and foraging easy.

Because the mammalian female is so specialized for parental care, most mammalian fathers, as I've said, have little to do with the raising of their young. Those that do help out, by protecting their offspring or by feeding them or their mother, have good reason to be sure of their paternity *and* they are able to make a substantial contribution. For this reason, paternal care in mammals is more common in those whose food comes in large, energy-rich packets that can be carried or stored for later use. When a pack of wolves kills a moose or a caribou, the wolves can save part of the meat by burying it; they can also bring food back to share with the rest of the pack by eating from the carcass, then regurgitating the partially digested meat. For the same reason, paternal care is extremely rare in herbivores, my sheep, for example, which rely on flight rather than fight for protection and eat grass, a sparsely distributed, low-protein, low-energy food.

An interesting exception to the lack of paternal care in most herbivores is the beaver. Beavers form long-term monogamous relationships, and male and female cooperate in raising the young. Young beavers stay in their parents' lodge for up to two years. Diet is certainly one of the keys to the beaver's family life. Trees, beavers' food, *do* come in large, energy-rich packets and *can* be stored for later use. The artificial ponds created by beavers are nothing more, in fact, than large storage facilities for trees and the nutritious bark that covers them.

Another example of a caring herbivore father, this time a grazer like the sheep, is the klipspringer or cliff hopper, a dwarf antelope, barely two feet high at the shoulder, that lives in the mountains of Ethiopia. Klipspringers are one of the most strictly monogamous mammals, even though the male is unable to feed or defend either his mate or his young. But what he does do is just as important to the survival of these solitary creatures, the prey of leopards, hyenas, and even baboons. He stands guard while his mate feeds. By serving as her eyes and ears, he allows her to concentrate on eating without having to check constantly for predators. Females also stand guard for males, but, because a lactating female spends twice as much time feeding as a male, guarding falls more heavily on her mate's shoulders. When neither is feeding it is usually the male who maintains vigilance. The female lets down her guard, thereby saving energy for the birth and nursing of their single fawn.

Among primates, males also play a wide variety of roles in the lives of their young. These range from the total indifference of squirrel monkey fathers to the hands-on caregiving of marmoset fathers. In this species of small South American monkeys, the male carries, grooms, and comforts his twin infants. He assumes almost complete responsibility for them, turning them over to their mother only for nursing and carrying them until their combined weight equals his own. Baboon males also carry and associate with infants, but their purpose is not so much to help the mother out; rather, it is to deflect aggression against them by other males or to increase their access to the mother. "He that wipes the child's nose kisseth the mother's cheek," George Herbert observed of humans, but his observation applies to other primates as well.

Most of these primates share the same, largely vegetarian diet, and their patterns of fathering can be explained, instead, on the basis of their paternal certainty, which derives in part from their social structure and relates to their ecology. Marmosets live in fairly small groups and feed on the fruit of small trees, which can be defended by one male. In this species, where "males tend to show an almost maternal solicitude toward infants," as the naturalist Edward Wilson observed, only one male (or very few males) is the possible father of any one infant. By contrast, baboons, chimpanzees, and squirrel monkeys live in large groups, and many males cooperate in defending their food resources, the fruits of large canopy trees. In these species, any one male is less likely to have fathered an infant, and interactions between males and infants usually serve ends other than caregiving.

In all the human cultures that have ever been studied, males have been found to take an extremely minor *direct* caretaking role in relation to children and, especially, infants. But in their *indirect* roles as economic providers and defenders of women and young, they are unsurpassed by any other primate—even the marmoset. The investment they make in their offspring, it can be argued, is equal to that of the human female, though it is of an entirely different kind. But because it is or has been indirect (in our culture, at least, fathers' roles are changing as mothers' roles change and women take on more responsibilities outside the home), it is sometimes overlooked or taken for granted.

Also overlooked is the role that paternal care played in human evolution. All the higher primates give birth to young that are somewhat premature or altricial at birth, but the human infant, as we have seen, is the most premature of all. His or her physical, cognitive, and social capabilities take decades to mature.

And it was fathers, fathers who provided for their mates and young, that allowed this to happen. The early human female could not have gone this way alone. Most primate females, primatologists will tell you, are at the very edge of their ability to provide for their young and themselves; they have great difficulty in finding food enough to sustain both lactation and their own body weight. In order for early humans to so amplify the trend toward altriciality, females needed to elicit support and energy from some other source. It was the presence and protection of fathers that allowed females to give birth to infants at an earlier and earlier stage of their development. These infants were, of course, increasingly helpless at birth and increasingly dependent on the devotion of their parents, but they made up for their slow starts with their amazing capacities for learning.

No one knows, of course, exactly how it happened, but at some point in human evolution, men discovered that they could raise more children if they provided food and protection for their mates than if they left their pregnant mates behind and looked for new wombs to fertilize. Likewise, at some point in human evolution, women found that they could do better if they chose to mate with males who would stick around, defending them against other males and against the swift predators of the African savannas, giving them the extra attention they needed in the event of a premature birth, adding to the food that they were able to forage on their own.

And so it happened. One male's protection and provisions of fish and rabbit and one female's choice of a mate who would provide led to healthy, smarter children who grew and throve and survived to have children of their own, who might, in turn, make good providers or good choices. A female's concealed estrus (her ability to mate at any time), her willingness to share her food with her mate, her ability to form and elicit strong attachments—to love and be loved—were all ways that she could attract and keep a mate for the very long time it would take her children to reach the point of independence. It was not a kind process. Natural selection does not know kindness. In all but very unusual situations, infants who did not receive extended care from both their parents did not survive; they did not have the chance to pass on any lack of caregiving genes or behavior.

Anthropologists like Margaret Mead used to wonder why the custom of marriage—a ritual in which one man and one woman are made husband and wife—is found in nearly every human society. Was it that marriage provides a way for men and women to share the products of their labors, a necessary pairing in a species in which labor is divided along gender lines? Or was it that marriage is society's way of putting the lid on competition between males, competition that is particularly intense because of the human female's ability to mate at any time?

But these anthropologists, it is now clear, were looking at marriage backward and upside down. Marriage is not imposed by laws or society but is, rather, an expression of the human tendency toward monogamy, a formalization of the human pair bond: formed in response to the needs of infants and contributing, in turn, to the evolution of those infants. No one knows exactly when this bond became part of the human makeup, but ever since Homo habilis and Homo erectus began to walk the African grasslands, some two million years ago, in all probability the male has been an essential part of the human family.

It may be that human males are monogamous by necessity rather than choice (in most parts of the world it is difficult enough to support one wife and family—never mind two),[4] but all animals that are monogamous, males and females, are monogamous by necessity rather than choice. That is just what it means to be a sexually reproducing animal. And why should we mind when necessity is so completely disguised and quickened by feelings of love and attachment, by the conviction that one cannot possibly live without one's mate?

None shall part us from each other,
One in life and death are we:

All in all to one another—
I to thee and thou to me!

Thou the tree and I the flower—
Thou the idol; I the throng—
Thou the day and I the hour—
Thou the singer; I the song!

Sir William Gilbert has two lovers sing in *Iolanthe*. Humans have been endowed with the physiology of love, the equipment they need to form the attachments that are necessary to give their children a good start in the world.

Yet, it can't ever have been easy for one man and one woman to stay together for the amount of time necessary to raise their young. If it was, our poetry, our songs would not also be so full of love lost and the disappointment of love. It can't ever have been easy, and certainly it is far less so today in industrialized societies, where men and women are not so critical to each other's survival—and the survival of their offspring—as they once were. The ties that bound us—male to female and parent to offspring—during thousands of years of hunting and gathering and hundreds of years of agriculture have slackened. At the same time, changes in sexual mores make mate guarding old-fashioned but do not address the fundamental engines that drive male parental behavior.

For as with all animals, human males do not provide care under just any circumstances. Paternal care is most pronounced, most predictable in the same circumstances in which all male care has evolved: when men are certain that the children they are caring for are their own (I will come to adoption later) and when men can make important contributions to their children's well-being. Crosscultural studies have tended to confirm this.

In an analysis of 186 preindustrial societies (present-day societies such as Somalia and Burma as well as ancient societies such as Egypt and Rome), sociologists Steven Gaulin and Alice Schlegel rated each society for paternal confidence on the basis of the presence or absence of traditions of extramarital sex and wife sharing. Then they examined the inheritance, succession, and residence patterns of each. In those societies where paternal confidence is or was high (the ancient Aztecs and Babylonians, and the Lapps, for example), they found that fathers did indeed direct their investments—their wealth, property, position, and day-to-day involvement—toward their wives' children. In societies where paternal confidence is or was low (the Fijians, Hurons, Ibo, and Romans), males tended to leave their wealth and titles to people other than their wives' children.

Other studies have shown that in human societies, males with the highest status, those who have accumulated the most power or heritable resources (and stand, therefore, the most to lose from being cuckolded), guard their mates much more closely than do lower status males, using claustration (confining women in cloisters), footbinding, infibulation (fastening the sexual organs with a fibula or clasp), virgin marriage, and chastity belts to do so.

Jane Lancaster, an anthropologist who has studied the evolution of the human family for many years, is now looking at patterns of paternal investment in America today and finding similar results. In Albuquerque, where she lives and works, Lancaster is asking men about their reproductive decisions. How did they decide how many children they would have? How much would they invest in those children? Did they think they would stay with one wife and her children or look for a second wife and form a second family?

According to Lancaster, the decisions that twentieth-century American fathers are making are very much the same as those that fathers—of all species—have always made. They are more likely to leave a partner if they are not sure the children are their own; they are more likely to leave if they are unable to make a substantial economic contribution to their children's welfare. "A lot of the breakdown of the American family," noted Lancaster when I called to ask about her work, "is based on a lack of opportunity for men who don't have advanced skills. These men are more likely to leave one partner and find another because they know that their children aren't going to be any better off if they stay."

And the problem with this, of course, is that while the reproductive behavior of human males and females changes in response to changes in the environment, the needs of human children do not. Children still need years and years of parental care. Their big brains still develop best in the context in which those brains evolved—the family. "Infants and children still fare much better," said Lancaster, "when they have the love and support of their two parents.

"Much better," she was quick to add, "unless they fare much worse," unless the family environment is so destructive that normal, healthy growth is impossible.

IV

The Art
of Nesting

In the Lila Acheson Wallace Bird House at the Bronx Zoo,[1] visitors are watching a pair of concave-casqued hornbills. These are large, colorful birds, natives of India and Sumatra, with enormous, curved beaks that look far too heavy for the birds to lift but are, in fact, made of a light, spongy material. Only the head of the female hornbill is visible; the rest of her is hidden inside a hole high up in the large artificial tree that occupies much of the exhibit. The male is perched on one of its branches. His beak rests on the rim of the hole; his head is cocked as if to better hear what is going on inside. His demeanor is one of rapt attention and total solicitousness. As I watch him, I am strangely moved. Although I consider myself a very lucky person, for I am loved by a number of people whom I love in return, I can count on one hand the number of times that someone has listened to me or looked at me like that.

Suddenly the male hornbill sits up, and his entire body begins to heave. He regurgitates a purple grape and holds it delicately at the end of his huge beak. He offers the grape to his mate in the hole. She accepts it in her beak, then passes it back to the male. Back and forth it goes until the male finally throws the grape up in the air, catches it, and swallows it. In a few minutes he hops down to the ground and comes back with a chunk of apple, which he also offers to his mate. They pass it back and forth, and this time she eats the morsel.

"This is like a soap opera. They're kissing," a woman says to her companion.

"He looks like a punk rocker," the companion replies. She might be talking about the bird's spiky plumage—black, orange, and white—or maybe his red eyes, like grapes themselves. The females look identical to the males except that their eyes are white.

The pair continue their courtship feeding, a behavior that is common in many birds, and especially monogamous species in which the male helps to feed the young. That is certainly the case with these hornbills—but with a twist.

After hornbill females lay their eggs in their nesting holes, they plaster themselves—and their eggs—inside, using materials brought to them by their mates (fruit, mud, excrement) and leaving just a narrow slit open for feeding and defecation. There they sit for the entire incubation period and much of the nestling period, for one to four months, depending on the species, until the young are so large that there is no longer room for the mother inside the cavity. She then breaks down the plaster wall and leaves to help her mate with the feeding and her young seal the cavity up behind her.

But during the time that the female is with her young inside the hole, the male has the sole responsibility for feeding them. If anything should happen to him or if the female has misread him and he is not the devoted male, the good provider, the solicitous partner that she took him for, she and her offspring may starve. We at the zoo were watching an exchange of fruit, of energy, the necessary stuff of eggs, but we were also watching an exchange of vows, a sign language of fidelity and devotion and a necessary prelude to hornbill breeding.

In between 1994's record number of snowstorms, I made my way back to the bird house to watch the hornbills' nesting progress. For many weeks there was no change that I could see. The female was inside the open cavity, sometimes preening herself, sometimes straining mightily, sometimes knocking her bill against the cavity wall. The male, ever devoted, was outside, sometimes watching her, sometimes feeding her, sometimes clashing bills with her, his head inside the cavity. Then one day the female was sitting outside her hole on a branch looking like nothing so much as a sullen, disappointed child. The male was on the branch of a second tree with his head deep inside a second cavity.

I telephoned Dr. Don Bruning, the curator of birds, to ask what had happened. He thought there had been an egg, but either it had been infertile or it had somehow broken. This pair hasn't been successful in several years, he said, though they had raised broods in the past.

Was it that they were too old? I asked, thinking of the male's dirty bill and shabby-looking feathers.

The female was over twenty years old, I was told, but that shouldn't have been a problem since this species of hornbill can easily live thirty or forty years. Dr. Bruning could not say exactly what had happened, but it was clear that nesting isn't always successful, even in the Bronx Zoo, where hornbills have no need to find food and no predators to fear, no reason to seal themselves inside trees. In the wild, their failure might have stimulated them to separate and look for new mates and new nests. In the zoo, they can only try again next year.

❧

Few animal parents take nesting to the extreme of the hornbills—excavating a cavity, then sealing themselves inside—but for many parents nesting and nest building are important parts of the care they provide their young, a critical first step in child raising. Protected places where parents can lay their eggs or leave their young while they forage for food or drive away a predator, nests make the jobs of parents a little easier. They improve the reproductive odds. Sometimes they do this so well that they also reduce the need for parents, and species of birds that build the most elaborate nests are often those in which one bird parents alone.

Each nest-building animal creates a structure of characteristic size and shape, using only certain materials and techniques, and each of these structures has been designed by evolution to meet the needs of the young and to lighten the energetic loads of the parents: to keep eggs and young warm in cold climates and cool in hot ones, dry in rainy places and moist in dry ones; to help parents avoid the attentions of predators while allowing them to be close to food and water.

The materials that animals use to build nests are as varied as the nests themselves, but each material has a precise function: thistle-down, feathers, moss, and grass for insulation; rootlets, sticks, and cobweb silk for structural support; lichens and bark for weather-proofing and camouflage. Availability is a major factor in an animal's selection of nesting materials, as are the needs of the offspring. In open country, many animals use fine grasses to line their nests because grass entraps a lot of air and is an excellent insulator, but in mountain forests, mosses and lichens are the insulation of choice. In very hot climates, ventilation and exposure to the sun are the problem. In these areas, nests are sited in the shade of trees and rocks and are rarely lined. The white-winged dove, which nests in the deserts of the southwestern United States, builds an extremely flimsy but extremely well-ventilated platform out of twigs. In the Antarctic, where no plant materials are available but where Adélie penguins must keep their eggs and nestlings above the water created by melting snow, nests are built out of small stones.

Nests are not static things, designed and then abandoned by the forces of natural selection. As circumstances change, nests and nest sites can also change. In places where there are few predators, birds that have always nested in trees may abandon this practice and save themselves the time and energy it takes to fly up and down to the nest site carrying building materials or food for their nestlings. Gardiners Island, a private island off the coast of New York, is home to very few cats, raccoons, and snakes, and its population of ospreys, birds that normally nest in the tops of trees and telephone poles, have given up their lofty perches for nest sites on the ground. There, they are that much closer to the fish that they feed on.

Animals construct their nests, some of them architectural wonders, with the only tools they have: their feet, beaks, teeth, paws, claws, and mandibles. A worker bee uses its head as a plummet so that its hexagonal cells will be precisely oriented to the line of gravity. Its antennae are the calipers that keep the waxen cell walls at a thickness of precisely 0.073 millimeters.

Birds have committed their forelimbs to flight, so the bill is their chief tool, and "it may be pressed into service," as Alexander Skutch, a noted ornithologist, has written, "as a chisel or drill for carving into wood, a pick for delving in earth, a shuttle for weaving, a needle for sewing, a trowel for plastering." The bee-eater, a small burrowing bird related to the kingfisher, begins its six-foot-long tunnel by flying directly into a bank or a riverbed with its bill partly open, a technique that sometimes knocks the bird out. The Indian tailorbird, a member of the warbler family, sews together living leaves with cobweb. Woodpeckers chisel out deep, smooth-walled cavities in living trees, and their heads are constructed so as to withstand percussions without injury to the brain's delicate structures. Their cavities are the envy of their avian neighbors and the cause of many disputes, evictions, and even murders. In the pine forests of the American South, at least nineteen species of animals try to appropriate the holes excavated by the red cockaded woodpecker.

Mammals use teeth, paws, and claws to dig the burrows and dens that they use as nests. The mole's enlarged forefeet are turned outward, enabling it to do a kind of breaststroke through the soil, to swim through porous ground at a rate of about one foot per minute. When the pocket gopher digs her burrow, using her large, well-developed incisors like a backhoe, her lips close behind her teeth, preventing soil from getting into her mouth. She uses her pockets (the large, fur-lined pouches on her cheeks) to bring in bedding for the nest, squeezing out their contents with both forepaws, then turning the pockets inside out to clean them.

Nest-building animals need a blueprint with which to build, and for this they also use their bodies. Scrapes, the simplest birds' nests, are made in much the same way that children make snow angels. Cup nests are molded to the maker's body, and even elaborate structures use the builder as a measuring rod, like the kidney-shaped, roofed nest of the Cassin's weaverbird. The dimensions of this nest are determined by the bird's reach as he stands on his foundation ring, the first part of the nest he builds.

Nurseries for the young, nests are also permanent records of animal behavior—3-D recordings of the hundreds of trips it might have taken to build them, trips in which animals went back and forth carrying sticks, straw, dung, or milkweed silk in their beaks, mouths, mandibles, or claws. Each nest is a kind of hologram of a particular animal's particular way of shaping these materials into a structure that will last for the time it is needed. A hologram of that animal's technique of felting, thatching, weaving, sewing, plastering, or papier-mâchéing.

I have before me my own small collection of these 3-D recordings, these frozen behaviors, animal nests that I collected when the leaves were down and I was suddenly aware that a pair of finches had been nesting in the clematis next to the back door or that mockingbirds had summered in the wisteria growing up the side of a small outbuilding. I even recognize some of the objects in these nests: sheep's wool, of course, now turning up in the nests of barn swallows, as well as in those of house finches and purple finches; a small piece of the string I use to tie up plants in the garden; hair, by the look of it, from my own head.

The yellow jacket nest that I retrieved from the branches of a dogwood tree is mostly gray, I know, because it is made of the weathered wood of our fence posts. This nest—a thin, spherical, paper envelope with a breeding comb inside—is truly wondrous. The yellow jackets fabricated the paper by shaving off minute pieces of wood with their jaws, then chewing up these pieces, mixing them with saliva, and spreading the mixture into thin sheets. The result is a beautifully patterned sheath of muted grays, browns, and tans. Each small arc of color, no more than an inch in length, represents one trip by one wasp carrying one load of wood cells from one source: gray arcs from the fence posts and telephone poles; reddish arcs from decaying oak trees. A single nest, capable of housing some 2,000 wasps, might be made of 200,000 such loads, 200,000 trips recorded like entries on a time sheet.

Animals that raise their young in nests must also keep those nests clean, for excrement attracts predators and is a breeding ground for parasites. Most small birds are fastidious housekeepers, searching the nest for foreign materials and periodically shaking the nest lining in a vigorous fashion. They deal with excrement in one of two ways. Passerines or perching birds collect it in their beaks as their young void and carry it away to some distant spot, but the young of other species simply turn their tails toward the rim of the nest and shoot their loads overboard. Hornbill mothers and their offspring, sealed inside their cavities for perhaps a hundred days or more, solve their hygiene problem by high-speed defecation through the slit, a kind of projectile vomiting in reverse.

Nesting mammals use similar methods to keep their nests clean. A mother dog is quick to notice when a pup begins to squat and quick to lap up the urine or feces with her tongue. When the pups are older, they will walk away from the litter to defecate. And, like most birds, mammals rarely use the same nest twice, thereby avoiding a buildup of parasites.

Some animals also take a preventive approach to parasites. Starlings incorporate green plants with known insecticidal properties into their nests, and nuthatches place pine pitch around the entrance holes to their cavities. The eastern screech owl keeps live blind snakes in its nest to eat the soft-bodied larvae that inhabit the nest's mess of fecal matter and uneaten prey. Snakes are usually the worst enemies of birds, but owl nestlings grow faster and have a lower mortality rate in nests with live blind snakes in them.

❦

Not all animals build nests, of course. The habit is rare in fish, reptiles, and frogs except among those species which show the greatest amounts of parental care. Insects are as famous for their nests as birds, but most insects do not, in fact, build nests, just as most do not show parental care. The insect's reputation for nest building comes mostly from the architectural feats of a small subset of insects—the social insects: ants, termites, bees, and wasps that live together in large groups and use vast workforces and sophisticated caste systems to construct nests of amazing size and complexity.

Because of the complexity of these nests and of the caste systems of their builders (in some species of ants and bees, individuals are specialized to serve as fans, ventilators, heating devices, door plugs, honey pots, and so on), it is easy to forget that, like all nests, these have been constructed for the sole purpose of providing a safe and nurturing home for insect larvae. The larvae are each nest's most precious commodity, and careful attention is given to their every need. In the breeding comb inside the wasp nest that I keep on my desk, larvae used to beg for food by rhythmically scratching on their cell walls (making a sound "not unlike the crunching of lettuce," as two biologists have observed), and they were fed mouth-to-mouth, mandible-to-mandible by special workers who brought them insects that they had chewed into a pulp. The larvae were kept warm, and the air in the comb was heated to precisely eighty-six degrees Fahrenheit by the muscular activity of other workers who acted as living furnaces, contracting and stretching their abdomens in rapid succession.

Ant nests can contain hundreds of thousands, even a million individuals, and these huge labor pools have given rise to more primitive methods of infant care. On a warm day, large numbers of ants will sit in the sun; then, when they are sufficiently baked, they will take their hot bodies down into the nursery to warm the eggs and larvae. Or, instead of heating the nursery, large numbers of ant workers will devote themselves to constantly moving larvae to the warmest parts of the nest.

With ants, bees, and wasps, it is also easy to forget that the complex, densely populated nests were started by a single female looking for a place to lay her eggs. The difference between these females and the females in the rest of the animal world is that, instead of laying eggs that hatch into fertile males and females, they lay eggs that hatch, usually, into sterile daughters. These daughters are the workers of the ant nests and beehives. Instead of reproducing themselves, they help their mother to lay even more eggs, and they care for those eggs and build a structure—a hive or a hill—where their mother will, eventually, lay eggs that hatch into fertile males and females.

What's in it for these sterile daughters, you might ask? Charles Darwin certainly did. The existence of these castes of nonreproducing workers was one of the reasons he held back for so long from publishing his theory of natural selection. Darwin was proposing that natural selection, best described as competitive reproduction, was the driving force of evolution and of all life. So sterile insects, as he once wrote, were the "one special difficulty which at first appeared to me insuperable, and actually fatal to my whole theory."

Darwin solved the puzzle of the sterile daughters in his own mind with the idea that natural selection could apply to the family and not just to the individual, that sterility among insects could evolve if the sterile workers were important to the survival of their fertile relatives. With this explanation he accounted for insect societies sufficiently well that generations of biologists were untroubled by their existence. He hadn't completely solved the puzzle, but he had managed to put it on a back burner until a time when advances in genetics would allow it to be solved.

Then, in the 1960s, as the British biologist William Hamilton began to work out the genetics of social insect societies, he came to a startling realization. Ants and those species of bees and wasps that live in large colonies are predisposed to sterility and to this kind of sisterly altruism, he realized, because of the way they inherit sex, because of their unusual method of sex determination which came to be called haplodiploidy.

Hamilton discovered that the males in these societies are haploid—they have, in all their cells, only one set of chromosomes. But the females are diploid—they have two, one from each parent, like humans and most other animals. And the females lay two types of eggs: unfertilized, haploid eggs, which develop into males, and fertilized, diploid eggs, which develop into females, either sterile workers or fertile queens depending on how they are raised.

The consequences of this mode of sex determination, Hamilton realized, were extraordinary. For instance, because the sisters in any one nest share the same set of genes from their father (he is haploid, remember, and only has one set to give), and half of their mother's genes, they are more closely related to each other than to either of their parents or any offspring that they might have. Sisters in diploid species share, on average, half their genes, but sisters in these haplodiploid species share three quarters.

Because of this, the insect worker's best reproductive strategy is to produce not offspring but, rather, sisters. To become not a mother, but a sterile worker that will protect and feed her own mother so that she will produce as many sisters as possible. The best reproductive strategy of these females is to make more of themselves. While it may look like they are unselfishly tending their mother's brood, they are, in fact, farming her for more sisters.

Hamilton had discovered the basis for the social insect's seeming altruism (all the ants, wasps, and bees that live in large societies have this mode of sex determination; all the wasps and bees that live solitary lives inherit sex in the normal way),[2] and in the process he began to greatly clarify Darwin's theory of natural selection. What counts is not just individual fitness, individual reproductive success, but inclusive fitness: the sum total of an individual's genetic legacy, taking into account children, siblings, cousins, and so on.

In order for an altruistic trait like ant sterility to evolve, Hamilton reasoned, its benefit to relatives must outweigh its loss to the altruist by a factor that is the inverse of the degree of relationship between the donor and the relative. For reproductive altruism among sisters to emerge in a diploid species, a sister has to more than double her sister's children to make up for the genes that she will lose to subsequent generations by not having children herself. For first cousins to help each other, the benefit must be eightfold. But ant sisters, as Hamilton discovered, must only increase the reproductive potential of their fertile sisters by one and a third.

The story doesn't end here, though. For when Robert Trivers looked at Hamilton's reasoning, he saw that it would only explain female sterility in ant societies if the sisters could somehow make their mother produce many more daughters than sons. Because of the haplodiploid method of reproduction, ant sisters share only one quarter of their genes with their brothers, so if the queen produced the normal fifty-fifty ratio of sons and daughters (something she is wont to do since she is equally related to her sons and daughters), there would, in fact, be no benefit to the sisters. The high degree of relatedness among sisters would be canceled out exactly by the very low degree of relatedness between sisters and brothers.

Because sisters are three times more related to one another than to their brothers, Trivers calculated that it was in the sisters' best genetic interest if the nest put three times more effort into producing females than into males. Trivers was only theorizing, but, when he and entomologists began examining the ratio of females to males in a wide variety of ant colonies, they found that theory matched fact. In colonies in which the queen had mated with only one male (queens can store sperm from several males, thus complicating enormously degrees of relatedness between sisters), the three-to-one ratio between sisters and brothers was almost exact. Sisters somehow manipulated their mothers into producing three times as many females as males.

It was this exactitude that made other biologists sit up and take notice. Genes certainly seemed to be dictating ant behavior. Could it be that they dictate other animal behavior as well? In the years since Hamilton and Trivers laid out their brilliant arguments, many forms of seeming altruism in animals—the adoption of a chimpanzee infant by another chimpanzee, the communal nursing of lion cubs, the cooperative breeding of some birds—have been found to involve closely related individuals, to be driven by genetic interests, the engine of inclusive fitness.

But does this mean that all animals, humans included, are completely selfish beings, intent only on their own reproductive futures, acting only in their own carefully calculated genetic interest? Does it mean that we are all out for self alone? To those living in bleak, war-torn, or disadvantaged communities, this may indeed seem to be the case, but most of us know that it cannot be the whole story. We know it from our own experiences: the thousand kindnesses that we have received from the hands of strangers, the heroic acts that we've witnessed, the need that many of us have to "give back" to the communities in which we grew up.

Trivers knew this too. He understood that genetic relationships alone could never account for the complex, often benevolent, social interactions of a troop of chimpanzees or a village of *Homo sapiens,* and though he was often criticized for placing too much emphasis on the role of selfishness in behavior, his very first paper, published in *The Quarterly Review of Biology* in 1971, was on how altruism outside of family groups could have evolved. He argued that all that was required for a species to develop the kind of altruism he dubbed reciprocal altruism, a tendency for unrelated individuals to help each other out, was that it be long-lived (individuals had to be around long enough to have the chance to pay each other back for any favors rendered) and that the individuals within the species be able to recognize one another (so that they could remember who had done what for whom and so that they could guard against cheaters or nonreciprocators) and spend most of their lives in the same place or the same group (so that the same individuals would see each other again and again). These criteria are met by many sea birds and large mammals that live in social groups, including, of course, humans.

So it is not that human beings haven't been shaped by natural selection but, rather, that we have been shaped in our own way. The human reproductive strategy depends not only on cooperation between individual males and individual females and their close kin but also on cooperation between bonded pairs. Because humans who banded together to hunt and share their knowledge about where edible plants could be found (to create increasingly predictable habitats and increasingly predictable food supplies) raised more children than humans who went it alone, banding together is as much a part of the human reproductive strategy as the pair bond or the helpless human infant.

Truly no man is an island. No man and his wife and his children are an island. Our first priorities may be our own children and kin, our own reproductive success and the accumulation of enough resources to ensure that success, but because we depend on one another, and on the social structure, for our reproductive success, we come with the capacity for friendship and the willingness (large or small, depending on circumstance and upbringing) to contribute to the social structure in ways that go far beyond paying taxes and making a living: preparing food for neighbors in times of need, serving as volunteer firefighters, sharing our expertise as lawyers, scientists, builders, and doctors.

Because humans, even humans that live in affluence, often voluntarily restrict the number of children they have, it is sometimes argued that we must be essentially different from other animals, that we must not be driven by the same genetic interests. But there is nothing in this behavior that sets us apart. *All* animals restrict the number of offspring they bear to the number they might successfully raise given the resources at hand. (And those animals that make the best predictions about resources have the best chance at long-term reproductive success.) In affluent societies, as the resources necessary to bring children to the point of independence and beyond—college tuitions, clothing, cars, down payments on houses—have gotten more and more expensive, in other words, scarcer and scarcer, our perceptions about the number of children we can raise have changed dramatically.

What sets humans apart is not the role genes play in our behavior but the number of relationships and attachments our big brains allow us to form, attachments that began with the infant's long-term need of care and the human female's long-term need of a mate and multiplied as the care of two parents allowed infants' brains to continue to grow. Even without haplodiploidy to dictate cooperation and social behavior, we are creatures who are very dependent on one another, creatures who have been made to give as well as to receive.

Unlike ants and bees, which have divided the job of reproduction into bearing (performed by the queen mother) and caring (performed by the sisters), humans have the primary responsibility of raising their own children; they usually care for those they bear. Our societies are not so inbred, after all, that we would share this important task. But human societies (like all animal societies) exist to make the jobs of parents easier. They exist to create stable environments in which parents can find the resources to live and work and provide for their young. If enough members agree, societies can also be made to take on some of the specific burdens of child raising—education, for example, or day care and health care.[3]

❦

Social insects, like ants and some bees and wasps, build elaborate nests because of their method of sex determination. Birds do it because they are warm-blooded and need a place to lay and incubate their temperature-sensitive embryos. The only birds that do not build some sort of a nest (if only a scrape in the ground) are the brood parasites, birds which lay their eggs in other birds' nests, and the birds that breed in places where nest materials are nonexistent—the sea ice of the Antarctic, for instance, where emperor penguins incubate their eggs on top of their webbed feet and inside special brood pouches—warm flaps that hang from the bellies of both sexes.

In order for normal development to occur, birds' eggs must be kept within a very narrow temperature range—thirty-four to thirty-eight degrees centigrade for most species. A bird's nest, therefore, is more than just a receptacle for a fragile embryo. Nest and bird together form the incubator that makes development possible. Birds and nests are two sides of the same coin, two halves of the same reproductive equation. Cavity-nesting birds like the hornbills often do little to improve upon their holes, but the trees provide effective insulation. When one curious ornithologist fitted a hornbill's nest with a temperature sensor, he found that, though the temperature on the tree's surface varied greatly in the course of one twenty-four-hour period, the temperature inside the nest changed very little. By day the thick walls of the tree trunk insulated the nest from the heat. By night heat stored in the walls flowed into the nest chamber.

The earliest birds probably buried their eggs, as crocodiles and megapodes do today, leaving incubation up to the sun. But as birds became warm-blooded, as they developed the ability to maintain a high and constant body temperature, natural selection would have favored those that sat on their eggs, especially on cool nights. Direct incubation of this sort would also have reduced the danger of nighttime predation and shortened the amount of time it took for the eggs to hatch. And it would have enabled birds to spread into colder regions that were relatively free from predators. These new regions, in turn, would have imposed new engineering requirements for nests, particularly in regard to their insulation value.

Though the nests of today's birds are probably the results of many sometimes competing environmental factors—temperature, predation, winds, climate, competition from other species—a few generalizations about them can be made.

- Since small birds have more difficulty maintaining their body temperature than do large birds (the surface area of a small bird is larger in relation to its volume so it loses more heat to the atmosphere), small birds tend to build the most elaborate nests. Among Old World birds, weaverbirds are noted for the variety and complexity of their nests. In the New World, tyrant flycatchers, ovenbirds, and orioles hold that distinction.

- Small birds are also less able to defend themselves and their young, so their nests tend to be well concealed. The delicate, lichen-studded cup of the ruby-throated hummingbird blends in so well with the branch on which it sits that it looks like nothing more than a knot in the wood. The orange-winged sitella, a nuthatchlike bird of Australia, shingles its nest with small pieces of bark in perfect imitation of the tree in which it builds. The bearded greenbul of the African rain forests works an epiphytic fern into the rim of its nest, and there the fern will stay green until just after the young fledge.

- Elaborate covered nests are far more common in tropical and sub-tropical regions, where builders are permanent residents, than at higher latitudes, where the majority of birds are migratory and cannot afford to devote as much time to building. Roofed nests may also be less common in the North because they don't allow birds and their nestlings to benefit from the early morning sun and more common in the tropics, where the threat from predators is so much greater. A nest with a roof prevents would-be plunderers from seeing what's inside.

- Form follows function. Birds like ducks and geese, with well-developed, precocial chicks that leave the nest soon after hatching, do not have the same need for sturdy nidifications as do birds whose helpless, altricial chicks will live in the nest for several weeks. Most birds with precocial chicks are ground nesters, and most ground nesters build simple nests.

Though acts of predation are rarely observed directly, even by bird-watchers who spend hundreds of hours in the field, ornithologists agree that predation has been the principal evolutionary force working on bird nests. Predation forced nests off the ground, and it forced birds to camouflage their nests and to breed in places that were less and less accessible: in thorn trees, as do the buffalo weavers of East Africa; in termite mounds, as do the white-tailed kingfishers of northeast Australia; on remote, rocky islands, as do many seabirds. It is also the force behind avian displays of cunning and duplicity, such as the sham doorway of the African penduline tit. This small bird makes a felted, hanging nest with a long spout that looks like it should be the nest's entrance, but is in fact nothing more than a fake door.

The real entrance is a trapdoor at the base of the spout. To open it, the tiny tit lands on the spout, seizes a flap of material, and pulls down. After entering the nest, the bird turns around and closes the trapdoor behind it.

Predation is also the force that brought birds together to nest in one tree or, like the sociable weaver of the South African savannas, to build great communal nests, where intruders might be mobbed or at least satiated before they wiped out every clutch. It is not that these birds agreed to sacrifice some for the good of the whole; simply, birds that clumped together left more offspring than those that did not.

To appreciate the role that predation plays in bird nesting, one need only know the statistics. In a study of fifty-three ant tanager nests in Belize, on the Yucatán Peninsula, 147 eggs were laid, but only 8 of the young escaped premature destruction. In a study of blackbirds in England, young birds fledged from only one out of every five eggs laid. No wonder the hornbill female seals herself in her nest and the rufous hummingbird is such a master at camouflage. No wonder the penduline tit makes two kinds of doors.

Where there are snakes, they are birds' greatest plunderers, slipping into the narrowest of cavities, sliding out to nests hung from the thinnest of branches. In the tropics there are even egg-eating snakes with teeth far back in their throats so that they can puncture eggs and eat the contents without losing a drop. But birds have many other enemies as well: other birds—hawks, owls, storks, jaegers, ravens, crows, gulls, jays, magpies—and all the carnivorous and omnivorous mammals—weasels, raccoons, humans, stoats, rats, foxes, coyotes, and mongooses. Even the largely vegetarian mammals—squirrels, monkeys, caribou, and sheep—do not turn their noses up at an egg. Birds may take to the air for most of their lives—for feeding, migrating, courting, and mating—but they must come down to earth, or at least to treetops, to lay and incubate their eggs, and there they lose all the advantages of flight.

To us, overworked but infrequently preyed upon humans, a bird's nesting period may seem like a quiet, relaxing time, but birds rarely doze when they are sitting on their nests, at least during the day. They are always alert, always on the lookout, always ready to make the decision whether to sit tight and hope that a passing cat or snake hasn't seen the nest or to fly off, distracting the marauder and/or saving their own skins. The bluebird female in my sheep field rarely flies out of her box when she is disturbed. Her sit-tight strategy keeps her from revealing the presence of her nest to those who do not already know of it, but it leaves her easy prey for the nighttime predator, the raccoon or black rat snake.

❦

Mammals, like birds, are warm-blooded animals, but nests are not so essential a part of their parental care because most mammals use their own heated bodies to incubate their embryos. This makes the nesting period shorter and less vulnerable for those mammals that do build nests. It also means that some mammals, those that give birth to well-developed young, can raise their young perfectly well without nests.[4]

The first year I had sheep, I wondered whether the ewes would want to build nests when it came time for them to give birth, and I put out extra straw and hay for them in case they did. I spent the next eight years mildly embarrassed that I ever could have imagined such a thing, but I know now that it really wasn't such an odd possibility after all. Nests pop up in strange places. Hoofed animals that are migratory do not build them, it's true, but hoofed animals that are territorial, like the pig, do. The pig's early labor is marked by frenzied nest building as the female roots out a shallow hole, then fills it with grass that she rips from the edge of the hole and scratches inside.

The big difference between pigs and sheep is that pigs give birth to altricial young, born naked and blind and initially unable to regulate their body temperature. Mammalian parents who have this kind of young rely heavily on nests to keep their offspring warm, and to keep them in one place and out of sight.

The burrow, as I've said, is the typical nursery of these kinds of mammals. More than half of mammalian species are rodents, and rodents tend to be expert diggers, excavating burrows of varying complexity and lining them with feathers, grass, or, in the case of the weasel, fur from a cottontail rabbit. Some of these rodents live underground year-round, but rarely do they give birth where they live. Rabbits and ground squirrels usually dig nesting sites away from the main colony. The Columbian ground squirrel takes great pains to conceal this birthing burrow, by opening the entrance from underground (so as to leave no telltale mound outside) and by leaving the burrow closed up for about four days before littering.

For most of the year, the harvest mouse lives underground, but before the female gives birth, she builds an aboveground nest that rivals those of many birds in daintiness and skill. Suspended from a stalk of corn, the nest is an apple-sized, woven ball of shredded leaves. Sometimes it doesn't have an entrance, a feature that puzzled naturalists until they discovered that it doesn't need one. Its construction is so elastic that the female simply enters through the walls. When the young grow so large that there is no longer any room for their mother inside the nest, they stick their heads out through the walls to nurse.

Felines tend to nest in caves and under natural cover, sometimes lining their nests with moss and foliage, but canines dig burrows. A study of Arctic wolves in East Greenland found that they often enlarged existing fox burrows to use as dens and that they always chose sites within fifty feet of a source of water, since lactating females need water every day. A few days before she gives birth, the female wolf pulls hair from her belly to line the underground nest, and she also buries food nearby for the first few days after birth. Her mate and the rest of the wolves in the pack will later regurgitate food for her and her young.

The beaver's lodge is one exception to the rule that animals do not live in the nests they build. This construction, a conical heap of sticks which houses a central living chamber, a ventilation shaft, and one or more underwater tunnels, is both nursery and home to the beaver pair and their offspring.

Beavers begin their lodge by simply piling sticks on top of one another. Then they plaster the outside walls with mud and stones, leaving the top two to three feet open for ventilation. Finally, they eat their way into the pile to make the entrances and the living chamber. The adults sleep on the floor of the lodge, but the young sleep in beds of grass and twigs arranged around the walls. When the beds are no longer needed, they too can be eaten. So can the store of twigs and branches piled up around the base of the lodge. The lodge is so well built that it can easily last a beaver's lifetime, which may be another reason why beavers are paired for many seasons, possibly for life. Stable structures and stable food supplies, it seems, help make for stable relationships.

Most primates have no need for nests because most primate mothers carry their young about with them at all times, and most primate young are born precocial in certain important ways: most are covered with fur at birth, and most are able to regulate their body temperature within a short time. Some primates build very simple nests in which to give birth. Chimpanzees may fold down a few leafy branches in the treetops just as they do every night when they make their sleeping nests; mountain gorillas may bend over grasses in a sheltered spot. But primates do not need nests in the ways most birds or wolves or mice need nests. They only need safe places in which to give birth.

This is true of apes, and it is also true of humans (the hairless human baby is kept warm by the use of clothing and by being held next to its mother), though one would not know it by the way the word *nesting* has crept into our vocabulary. For many women who have experienced childbirth, nesting refers to a time and a behavior almost as distinct and memorable as birth itself, a time when the lethargy of pregnancy gives way to incredible energy; a time when the refrigerator has to be cleaned out, the closets straightened, the clothes mended, the wallpaper hung, the furniture painted; a time of unusual focus on the house and the room where the baby will sleep. Only when I lined all the drawers with paper and finished knitting a small blue sweater and cap did I consider myself ready for the birth of my first daughter.

So what does this behavior mean? Is it the leftover tug of primal nest-building instincts, remnants of our distant evolutionary past, when small mammals were trying to survive the Ice Ages by digging burrows and building warm nests for their young? Or is it something else? Something particularly human?

One day I asked Dr. Wenda Trevathan, an anthropologist who has written extensively about mammalian birth, about this. In preparation for her book *Human Birth: An Evolutionary Perspective,* Trevathan had worked for a year as a midwife at a birth center in El Paso, Texas, and there she had heard all kinds of stories about the unusual behavior of women who are about to deliver.

"I can only speculate," she said. "But it must have been important for a woman who was about to go into labor to find a safe, quiet place to deliver. This restlessness must be a very basic instinct for all mammalian females. What differs—according to what species you are and what part of the world you live in—is what you consider safe. A burrow is safe for a rabbit. A tree is safe for some primates. For humans in warm climates, a safe place to give birth might be a bed of grass not far from camp. In colder areas, a safe place is a cave or a shelter.

"In our culture, though," she continued, "we don't choose where we want to give birth in the sense of creating a space. We choose by selecting a hospital and a doctor. So perhaps some of those preparations for the birth site—this nesting behavior or instinct, if you will— are coming out in other ways: cleaning, painting, and the like. What wouldn't make sense is that women would just sit around before they gave birth. It's hard for me to imagine that would ever be part of the picture."

We humans certainly go about some things differently. We build homes, not nests, and we live in these homes year-round. We live in the place where we raise our offspring, but we no longer give birth in that place, preferring the safer confines of a hospital. Yet, for all that, we are not that far removed from the hornbill sealing herself inside the tree or the harvest mouse weaving her ball of leaves. We are all trying to make a vulnerable time a little less vulnerable.

Egg Layers and
Live Birthers

There is an inevitability to raising livestock and to farm life that is maddening but also instructive. The barn or the sheep shed is the birthplace of the logical consequence, the first home of cause and effect. If you do not feed your animals right, they will sicken, die perhaps, and leave you with nothing but a large veterinary bill. If you ignore a hole in your fence, your

animals will certainly not. They will escape through

77

it and into your neighbor's garden, precipitating chases, confrontations, even a visit to small-claims court. On a farm, the piper always gets paid. *First.*

Don't think that this is an example of Murphy's Law: "Anything that can go wrong will go wrong." For it isn't. Murphy's Law is a law of businesses, of human affairs, and, in a world populated by people, things go wrong despite efforts to make them go right. On a farm, things go wrong because animals have twenty-four hours a day, seven days a week, in which to test fences and gates, in which to seek out the poisonous plants you failed to eradicate from your fields, in which to work their heads through chicken wire so they can eat every bud the peonies produce, every blueberry left by the squirrels. It is as if a business had a spy in it with nothing to do but find ways to undermine the operation. No pretenses to keep up. No legitimate front to maintain. Livestock, the subversives that some of us choose to live with, will always find our weaknesses and expose them. I guess they're a little like children in that way. But without the great, emotional rewards of children, the love and affection that children inspire.

During the winter of 1993–94, when seventeen snowstorms were piling up three to four feet of snow in our fields and driveway, I relearned these lessons the usual, hard way. By late December, the snow was so deep that we couldn't open the gates to our fields, and Jeff Traver couldn't deliver hay. For the rest of the winter, I had to buy hay from local feed suppliers. But they, too, were having difficulty with deliveries, and sometimes I was so desperate for something to give the sheep that I had to sweep up loose hay from their otherwise empty trailers. Usually, I fed the sheep in the middle of the field, on top of a hillock where we would later plant squashes and pumpkins, but as the winter progressed and I tired of the trek through the ever-mounting snow and ice, I took the simpler expedient of throwing the hay over the fence.

What I didn't consider was the effect that this new regimen would have on our black-and-white Border collie, a devoted but untrained sheepdog who spends most of his days watching the objects of his desire from a position just outside the fence. Now the sheep were feeding within a foot or two of his nose, so close that he must have been able to feel the heat rising from their woolly bodies. He managed to contain his excitement until the twelfth snowstorm or so. By then the plow had piled the snow so high on his side of the fence that the only thing keeping him from the sheep was habit. All he had to do to join them, to engage them in a game of tag, a round of nip and tuck in the deep snow, was simply walk over the once four-foot-high fence. One day when I was out on a quest for more hay, he realized this, and, when I returned home, the sheep were in a huddle near the pin oak and one ewe's ear was bloody and torn. The dog was crouched, fifteen feet away, watching intently from inside the fence.

And there we were in the dark later that night, my husband and I, scuttling around like crabs on snow coated with a thick layer of ice, trying to catch the pregnant ewe to examine her, wash her ear, and give her a tetanus shot. One minute we were playing our own game of tag, the next my husband had slipped on the ice and was flying through the air. He came down right on top of the nipped sheep.

Both my husband and the ewe survived the landing, and luck seemed to be heavily on our side in this particular round of logical consequences. The ewe's ear healed very quickly, and I didn't give much thought to her until she delivered in April, on the morning of the same day that the yearling walked away from her lamb, the morning of my husband's birthday. The nipped ewe didn't need any help in delivering, and she gave birth to two live lambs. But one of these lambs was enormous, a twelve-pound male, and one was tiny, a four-pound female. Both lived, but only because I helped the female lamb to nurse for several days, giving her exclusive access to her mother's teat and preventing her big brother from knocking her off her feet. And as I sat with them in the lambing pen, I had to wonder whether that ewe lamb was the end result of a chain of events that had begun with the fifth snowfall or so.

On the other hand, perhaps this tiny lamb would have been born this way if no snow had fallen last winter, if no dog had disturbed her mother's placid pregnancy, if no man had landed on her mother a little more than a month before she was due to deliver. Runts, after all, are fairly common fixtures of farms, and even fiction. Wilbur, the pig in E. B. White's *Charlotte's Web,* was a runt whose life was saved first by the tenderhearted Fern and later by an inordinately clever spider.

The dictionary defines *runt* as an animal that is unusually small compared with others of its kind. That definition covers the physical aspect of runts, but it doesn't answer the question of why they exist. From a Darwinian perspective, why would an animal spend its time and energy—its valuable reproductive resources—on an offspring so small that except in extraordinary circumstances (the ministrations of Fern in *Charlotte's Web* or my own interventions on behalf of the ewe lamb), it is doomed from the start?

The British ornithologist David Lack's pioneering work on clutch size in birds goes a long way to answering this question. Just as mammals give birth to a certain number of young, a characteristic litter size (one or two lambs for most sheep), birds of the same species tend to lay the same number of eggs. Eastern bluebirds lay four or five; house wrens lay six to eight. Ornithologists had long recognized that this was true, but before David Lack cast a Darwinian light on the matter in 1947, they had not understood why.

In one popular pre-Lack theory, clutch size was thought to represent a kind of avian birth control, with birds limiting the number of eggs they lay so that the birthrate of a species would match the mortality rate and the species would not overexploit its resources. Clutch size, in this view, is carefully adjusted so that each pair of adults produce in their reproductive lifetimes just enough offspring to provide replacements for themselves. This is the view that many of us grew up on: a pair of bluebirds or fish or wolves have just enough offspring that two will be likely to survive.

It's easy enough to smell the rat in this argument today, when most of us have at least a passing familiarity with sociobiology and the theory of the selfish gene. There is simply no mechanism by which natural selection can act on a species as a whole. Natural selection can only act on individuals and individual behavior. But when Lack first began looking into the rationale of clutch sizes, the theoretical landscape was fairly desolate. No one had even tried to apply Darwin's theory of natural selection to an actual instance of animal behavior.

Lack started with the assumption, novel at the time, that the "clutch-size of each species and local population has a hereditary basis, and that the number of eggs involved is ultimately determined by natural selection," as he wrote in a paper in the journal *Ibis*. He was also very aware, from the fact that most birds can replace a clutch if it is removed or destroyed, that birds produce far fewer eggs than they are capable of producing. "The limitation of clutch-size must be regarded not as a negative, the inability to produce more eggs," wrote Lack, "but as a positive act, the cessation of laying."

What causes this cessation? Lack dismissed population control on a species level for reasons I've already noted. And, from extensive field observations, he also dismissed explanations based on the age of the bird and/or its physical condition. He was left with the simple proposition that clutch size is a direct reflection of the parent birds' ability to find enough food to feed their young. On the one hand, a bird could always lay so few eggs that it was sure to be able to raise all its nestlings, Lack explained, but this would be an inefficient use of its reproductive time. On the other hand, if it laid too many eggs, and a number of nestlings starved, much of its parental effort would be wasted. Clutch size, Lack proposed, is a compromise between these extremes. It represents the average maximum number of young the parents can successfully raise in one season.

This seems so obvious in retrospect, but most of Lack's contemporaries thought that food supply was irrelevant to behavior. Lack's paper, though, immediately made sense of many avian peculiarities.

Clutch size increases with increasing latitude, Lack reasoned, because at higher latitudes the days are longer during the summer, when birds breed, so birds have more time to gather food. Those birds that raise two or three clutches in a single season lay smaller clutches in early spring, larger ones in June, and smaller ones thereafter. This pattern, too, is a reflection of the number of daylight hours, for in June day length is at its peak. Lack was also able to explain why the clutches of precocial birds tend to be so much larger than those of their altricial counterparts. Ducks can incubate up to twenty eggs at a time because they rarely feed their young; they only guide them to food. It is no coincidence, Lack made clear, that the megapodes of Australia, which have absolutely nothing to do with their young after hatching, set the record for clutch size. They can incubate thirty-four eggs in one season.

To understand just how much sense Lack was able to make of birds' egg-laying behavior, consider the European cuckoo. The cuckoo lays one egg in the nest of a much smaller species, redstarts, for example, or white wagtails. Upon hatching the cuckoo nestling throws all the legitimate eggs and nestlings out of the nest. Why? If Lack is correct, it is because one cuckoo is all that the adoptive parents can raise, and natural selection has favored those cuckoo chicks that refused to share the attentions of their adoptive parents with any of their foster siblings. Now consider this: the cuckoo fledges at a weight of 90 grams, a brood of six redstarts at 93 grams, a brood of five to six white wagtails at about 110 grams. No wonder Lack, who was decades ahead of his time, has been called "the chief architect of the selfish gene theory of family planning."

What does this have to do with sheep and runts? you might ask. I will come back to them, but first we need to look at some of the problems birds run into when they are planning their families. Because so many factors affect food supply—temperature, rain, cloud cover, storms, and so on—Lack also recognized that it would be extremely difficult for birds to judge precisely how many eggs they should lay, and he proposed that they might have evolved ways to bring clutch size and food supply into closer correspondence.

Asynchronous, or staggered, hatching in owls and hawks is one such method. Unlike most birds, which begin incubating their eggs only after they have laid their entire clutch, owls and hawks begin incubating after laying their first egg. Their chicks, therefore, hatch at long intervals, and the older ones have a big advantage when it comes to begging for food. In years of great abundance, the parent owls and hawks might be able to raise all the chicks. But in years when food is scarce, the youngest will quickly starve to death.[1] Chronism, named after the Titan Chronos, who devoured all but one of his own children, is another such method and is practiced by white storks (the birds we humans often picture in the role of midwives) as well as herring gulls, frigate birds, and the South Polar skuas.

While litter size in mammals is complicated by the fact that mammalian mothers incubate their eggs inside their bodies and give birth to live young, it has also been suggested that mammals adjust their brood size to food supply by eating part of their litter at birth, as some rodents do, or by producing runts: small investments that may pay off in a good year but will otherwise fall quickly by the wayside.

The decision to produce a runt or an extra egg is not, of course, a conscious one. Rather, those parents, mammals or birds, that make this gamble have tended to leave slightly more progeny than those that have played it completely safe. Whether they be the bluebirds that lay six eggs instead of the customary five or four, or the sheep that produce triplets instead of twins or single lambs, these parents are not so successful that the larger clutch or litter size becomes the norm but successful enough so that the gene or genes for producing these small gambles remain in the population. My tiny ewe lamb put on weight rapidly but never caught up to her brother. Was she the result of her mother's indecision—on some deep, physiological level—as to whether it was best to have one lamb or two? Or was she the outcome of that unfortunate tumble in the snow? Or is there yet another reason?

Mammals, as we have seen, incubate their eggs inside of them. They carry their developing young with them, and all animals that do this, whether in a uterus like mammals, an external brood sac like some insects, or a mouth like species of cichlid fish, have also to consider weight and mobility in calculating brood size.

Lack didn't discuss the constraints that arise from giving birth to live young (viviparity) because all birds are egg layers. In general, though, animals that incubate their young inside their bodies make a substantial trade-off between the number of offspring they can produce and this increased commitment to parental care. Viviparity is another step in parental care that trades quantity for quality. By giving developing embryos the protection of their own bodies and the benefits of a homogeneous environment, parents greatly increase their likelihood of survival but decrease the number of offspring they can produce.

Because most animals either produce eggs or bear live young, scientists can usually only speculate as to the benefits of viviparity. In one species of thrips, though, a minute insect that is responsible for much of the crop damage in this country, females can either lay eggs or give birth to live young. Not surprisingly, viviparous thrips produce only one half as many young as do egg-laying thrips. The young they produce, though, are twice as likely to survive to the pupal stage.

Egg laying may be the most common form of reproduction throughout the animal kingdom, but viviparity has evolved so many times and in so many animal lines—insects, mollusks, reptiles, fish, amphibians, and mammals—that it is clearly an effective trade-off, a highly successful reproductive strategy. When is it likely to evolve? It is most common in animals living in environments that vary greatly in some respect—temperature, for example, or oxygen levels—and in animals that face high levels of competition, predation, or parasitism. Among beetles, for instance, several viviparous species live inside ant or termite colonies where their eggs would be recognized as foreign and would be eaten or destroyed.

Viviparity has allowed other animals to colonize new habitats. The aquatic rag worm is usually restricted to salt or brackish water because its eggs die in freshwater, but a Californian rag worm is viviparous and can breed in both fresh and salt water.

In amphibians, viviparity reduces the danger of eggs and tadpoles drying out, and in some species, it has another important advantage: It allows embryos to grow at a discontinuous rate. Some frogs become pregnant during the dry season, but their embryos only start to develop during the rainy season, when the parent begins to feed. For mammals, too, discontinuous growth can be an advantage. The fertilized egg of a spotted skunk floats free in the uterus for several months before it becomes implanted in the uterine wall and full-scale development begins. This means that the skunk can mate in the summer or fall and give birth in spring, when food is plentiful and the conditions for survival are optimal. For some seals delayed implantation allows mating and birth to take place at the same time of the year, the one and only time the seals congregate ashore.

Given the number of times that live birth or viviparity has evolved in different animal lines and the advantages it does offer, we might well wonder that it is unknown among birds. All 9,000 species of birds use the same method of reproduction: They all lay eggs. And this is despite the fact that birds practice internal fertilization (they have taken that first, important step toward egg retention). The only exception here, and it is but a partial exception, is the parasitic cuckoo, whose eggs begin their development inside their mothers, an adaptation that gives cuckoo chicks a head start on their foster siblings.

Scientists have suggested many possible explanations for the lack of viviparity in birds, including the difficulties of flying when pregnant and the high temperatures of adult birds relative to their young. But bats give the lie to the argument that viviparity and flight are incompatible, and the temperature differential would not seem to be insurmountable. So the question still exists of why no birds give birth to live young. Or it did until 1986, when Daniel Blackburn and Howard Evans, ornithologists at Vanderbilt and Cornell universities, approached it from an entirely different point of view in a paper in *American Naturalist.*

"The literature is replete with statements to the effect that all birds lay eggs because as a group they are 'unable' to achieve viviparity," Blackburn and Evans observed. "The obvious alternative—that egg retention and viviparity might confer no net benefits on birds—is seldom considered."

To view viviparity as an inherently superior pattern reflects a strong mammalian bias, Blackburn and Evans suggested, and it might be that birds achieve through egg laying and biparental care the benefits that other animals get through viviparity. Birds are specialized for complex parental care and egg incubation, and though these specializations are not inherently incompatible with viviparity, the ornithologists pointed out, they greatly decrease the potential advantages of retaining eggs while magnifying the disadvantages. These include a loss in fecundity, an increase in maternal mortality, and, most significant perhaps, a decrease in paternal investment stemming from the fact that paternal certainty will decrease and fathers might well have separated from their mates by the time birth takes place.

The emperor penguin exemplifies what birds would give up if females were to incubate their eggs inside their bodies, for one would be hard-pressed to find fathers that do more for their offspring. In the dark of the Antarctic winter, when temperatures may drop to minus sixty degrees Fahrenheit, male emperor penguins, in groups of 7,000 or so, huddle together on sheets of sea ice. Each holds an egg, tucked in tight between the top of its feet and its warm brood sac.

On the sea ice there are no predators to disturb the penguins' incubation—no slithering snakes, no marauding birds. There the only enemy is the fierce cold, and the penguins shuffle about to stay warm. Males on the periphery of the group try to edge their way into the warm center, but this maneuvering takes some skill—especially with an egg balanced on one's feet. The stakes of a misstep, a tumble, are high. While the eggs of most birds can tolerate a brief chill and the absence of their parents for fairly long intervals, one minute of separation and the embryo inside the penguin egg will freeze. On particularly cold days, the penguins crowd together tightly; on warmer days, the mass opens up.

For two months, the male emperor penguin huddles thus, without eating, incubating its egg by burning the thick layers of fat it has put on in preparation for this long vigil. Its mate is far away at sea, replacing the pounds she lost in egg laying. If all goes well, the mother will return with a cropful of fish just when the chick hatches and is hungry for its first meal. But if something—an encounter with a leopard seal, unusual weather, a scarcity of fish—slows the female down, the male will have to abandon the chick and see to himself.

The penguins' synchrony is good, but it is far from perfect, and the sea ice of a penguin rookery is littered with abandoned eggs and dead young. Even *with* the devotion of two parents, 80 to 90 percent of the young will die between the time the eggs are laid and the time the chicks undergo their first molt.

❦

For animals that have taken the viviparous route, one key to live birth is that embryos must be retained within the body for a long time. In mammals this has meant the evolution of delicate hormonal clock pieces that maintain progesterone levels throughout gestation and inhibit contractions until the fetus can survive outside on its own. Gas exchange is also a problem that had to be solved, and researchers have suggested that the placenta evolved first as an organ for gas exchange and only secondarily, in large mammals, as an organ to nourish the embryo.

Other viviparous animals have very different ways of feeding their developing young. Early birth followed by a long period of lactation is the way of marsupials, mammals that lack a placenta and whose young are born, therefore, soon after the yolk of their eggs is used up. Female tsetse flies secrete a milky substance that is absorbed, through the mouth, by their single larva as it develops in the uterus. They give birth to that larva just before its second molt. One alpine salamander releases twenty to thirty eggs from her ovaries, but only one or two of these are fertilized. The rest degenerate into a kind of yolk that is eaten by the developing young after they have finished their own yolks. Great white sharks produce numerous eggs that develop and hatch inside the mother's womb (technically they are neither live birthers nor egg layers but some combination of the two), and after hatching the young remain in the womb for some time, feeding on one another.

Viviparity may be enormously beneficial to the young, but it is not without its costs for parents. It increases the energetic demands of parenting and the dangers parents face. For cold-blooded mothers that give birth to young sometimes weighing more than the mothers themselves, this is particularly true. A reptile like the Florida pine snake may refuse to eat when pregnant and may be noticeably hindered in her movements. Even mammals, though, which have managed to reduce the size of their eggs and developing embryos, experience trouble—especially during the last stages of pregnancy and especially if they are tree-dwelling mammals. When our primate ancestors moved up into the treetops, pregnant females must have found it difficult to move quickly through the branches. Large litters became a serious, insurmountable problem, and natural selection responded by reducing litter size in most primates to a single birth and by postponing much of the growth and development of the young to the postnatal period. Human infants still carry the results of that adaptation to arboreal life. Most are solitaires, and all do most of their growing after birth.

At the same time that pregnant mammals have sacrificed some of their mobility to offer protection to their growing young, they must continue to nourish themselves and their offspring. The energetic demands of the developing embryo increase through pregnancy, and the mammalian mother must meet those demands by eating more, eating more often, and eating food of better quality. Sometimes she takes considerable risks to do so.

Studies of animals in the wild have found that pregnant ewes, as well as pregnant moose and caribou, trade safety for food with a higher nutritional content as their pregnancies progress. They gravitate toward lowland areas, where young, protein-rich grasses grow but where the chance of meeting a bobcat, lion, or coyote is much higher. There they are particularly vulnerable to these predators since they have lost some of their speed and agility. After they have given birth, they again shift their feeding sites, now trading nutritional content for protection by taking their offspring high into the hills. During pregnancy sheep and other herbivores also become extremely picky eaters, seeking out those plants that best satisfy their increased needs for protein, minerals, and vitamins.

The pregnant female's ability to find these foods, it is now known, has serious consequences for her health, the health of her offspring, *and* her genetic future. On the small Scottish island of Rhum, the evolutionary biologist Tim Clutton-Brock studied a population of approximately three hundred wild red deer over the course of their entire reproductive lives. He found that red deer calves born below the average birth weight were more likely to die during their first winter. That in itself wasn't too surprising, but he also found that if these small calves did survive, they were more likely to bear small, light young throughout their lives and to lose a high proportion of these young before they reached maturity.

Since then similar effects have been documented throughout the animal kingdom. In coho or silver salmon, there is a close correlation between the size of a female's eggs, the early growth of her hatchlings, and their ultimate adult size, which is in turn closely correlated with increased fecundity, larger egg size, greater nest survival, and increased reproductive output. Big fish, in other words, lay big eggs, which hatch into big hatchlings, which produce more eggs over the course of their lifetimes. In humans, too, chronically underfed women have babies with low birth weight, babies more likely to be ill or to die than are the babies of women who have been adequately nourished throughout their lives. Supplementing a woman's diet during pregnancy will have only a slight effect on fetal growth or health (though it may compensate for some specific deficiencies). Fetal health and growth, it has been found, are largely dependent on the mother's nutritional state before pregnancy.

So the first job of parents is to stay healthy, maintain a good body weight, and bear good-sized young. If they are egg layers, the first job is to lay good-sized eggs. I don't know why it took me so long to appreciate this essential component of parental care. Probably because food in America is so readily available that fat is now something to struggle against, not for.

For most animal parents, staying healthy is their only job. For others, it is just one of many tasks, but the most fundamental by far, the most important dowry they will give their young and the best guarantee of their long-term reproductive success. In emperor penguins, the fattest males, those that can hold out longest in anticipation of their mates' return, make the best fathers. In many species, one female's talent at finding food and putting on weight translates into large eggs or offspring and cascades down through the generations.

The effect of birth weight on reproduction was not all that Clutton-Brock found in his fifteen-year study of the red deer. He had gone to Rhum to test one of Robert Trivers's most iconoclastic ideas—that certain mammalian mothers should be able to select the sex of their offspring—and had found that, for red deer at least, Trivers was correct.

The mothers that Trivers and the mathematician Dan Willard had in mind when they published another purely theoretical paper in *Science* in 1973 ("Natural Selection of Parental Ability to Vary the Sex Ratio of Offspring") were quite particular. A species would have to meet several criteria in order to show sex biasing, a change from the fifty-fifty probability of having female or male offspring that exists in much of the animal world.[2] Mothers in good condition had to be better able to bear and nurse young than mothers in poor condition so that the healthiest, strongest, heaviest offspring would be the offspring of the healthiest mothers. Also, there had to be some tendency for differences in the condition of the offspring to be maintained into adulthood (exactly what Clutton-Brock found for red deer). The final criterion was that differences in physical condition should affect male reproductive success more strongly than female reproductive success. This criterion would be met by all those polygamous species, like caribou and deer, in which males compete for mates and the strongest males exclude others from breeding and impregnate many females. The healthiest females in these species are able to invest more in their young, but because they can only give birth to one or two young per breeding season, they show, at best, only a moderate increase in reproductive success.

Trivers and Willard argued that if a species meets all these criteria, individuals should show evidence of sex biasing for compelling genetic reasons. In such a species, a female in good condition that produces a son will leave more surviving grandchildren than one that produces a daughter. Likewise, a female in poor condition that produces a daughter will leave more surviving grandchildren than one that produces a son. In the population as a whole, these biases or preferences will cancel each other out, but they should be evident to scientists who conduct painstaking long-term studies of banded individuals.

Trivers and Willard's hypothesis was met with considerable skepticism, and many of the biologists who headed out to the field to test it went with the idea of proving it wrong. Most wound up converts instead. In one study, opossum females that were given additional rations during pregnancy produced one and a half times the number of sons as did females fed a normal diet. In the same study, aging opossum females in poor health were twice as likely to give birth to daughters as to sons. In another study, fat, healthy nutria (polygamous, aquatic mammals native to South America) were found to selectively abort small, mostly female litters. And year after year on the isle of Rhum, red deer mothers in good condition gave birth to more sons than daughters. Red deer mothers in poor condition gave birth to more daughters than sons.

No one knows how it is done, at what point the bias occurs, but the results are unequivocal. All the mothers in these studies were able to skew their offspring toward the sex that was likely to provide them with the most grandchildren. Animals, it seems, are like futures traders; they have been selected to recognize a reproductive edge and to play it for all it's worth. And in nature, as Trivers suggested, no reproductive edge is left unexploited.[3]

Trivers and Willard proposed one particular circumstance in which sex biasing is likely to occur. Since publication of their controversial paper, biologists have discovered different circumstances, and they have found that sex biasing can also occur in the opposite direction. In some species, mothers in the best condition select for females rather than males. This happens where female reproductive success varies more than male reproductive success, where a female's rank, for instance, matters more to her daughters than to her sons.

In baboon and macaque societies, young males disperse after adolescence, but young females stay with their mothers, assuming a rank, or social position, just below their mothers'. A high rank guarantees access to food and freedom from harassment from other baboons. It means a female can begin to bear children at an earlier age than her lower-ranking counterparts and can bear more children over the course of her lifetime.

Is it surprising, then, that by some as yet unknown method high-ranking baboon mothers have many more daughters than sons? Low-ranking mothers have many more sons than daughters, for sons have a chance, at least, to work their way up in the baboon world.

❧

Thus we see that for some mammalian females the gestation period is a time to make adjustments in the sex or number of their offspring. For many it is also a time to adjust to the idea of offspring themselves and to their impending status as mothers. For those animals that live solitary existences, this is a big adjustment indeed, for they must overcome their normal inclination to either attack or flee another creature like themselves.

In many species, responsiveness to young develops over the course of pregnancy. When female rats breed for the first time, they become solicitous of other rat pups as they enter the last stage of their short pregnancy. Only then are they likely to bring wandering pups back to a nest site and to adopt a characteristic nursing posture. Squirrel monkeys begin to respond to infants two weeks before their due date and rhesus monkeys only in the last three days. But in primate species where communal or male care of infants is common, animals do not need to go through the physiological events of pregnancy in order to be interested in infants. All the members of marmoset troops are fascinated by newborns and vie for the privilege of holding and grooming an infant.

Human females do not seem to develop an interest in babies in general during pregnancy, but they do, over the course of their nine-month gestation, invest more and more of their emotions in the particular infant growing within them. In several studies, women interviewed during their first trimesters said that they had no image of their fetuses and had few feelings of warmth and attachment (though they did worry about a miscarriage). But by the last trimester, these same women often fantasized about their babies and were engaged in extensive preparations for their arrival. Their mates, without hormonal priming or a nine-month gestation, would also be engrossed by the infant by the time it arrived, and studies have shown that males and females behave in much the same way when presented with their newborns.

For the human female, pregnancy is also an energetically costly time (causing the mother to expend some 80,000 extra calories), when, like the ewe or the red deer, she must make every bite count, a vulnerable time that humans have tried to make less vulnerable by a long list of things that women should and should not do when they are pregnant.

Pregnancy may have more dos and don'ts, more taboos associated with it than any other event in a human's life. For women in industrialized societies, the taboos involve alcohol and drug consumption and certain kinds of exercise. Elsewhere they can be extremely esoteric. Weaving is proscribed in many cultures because it is thought to cause knots in the umbilical cord, a belief recorded as fact by Aristotle and the ancient Greek physician Galen. The Navajo also prohibit the hanging of laundry and the tying of other objects. Even braiding ropes and sitting cross-legged are thought to be dangerous. Some Japanese believe that if two pregnant women occupy the same house, one will die in childbirth, and in many cultures strong emotions are to be avoided at all cost. Excessive anger will cause a miscarriage or poison the milk, Mexicans say; any agitation can cause knots in the umbilical cord.

According to anthropologists, many of these taboos have their basis in the sympathetic magical beliefs of contagion or similarity, but surely they are rooted also in the nature of pregnancy and the nature of human beings. For pregnancy is a precarious state with a questionable outcome, and human beings are self-conscious creatures with long memories. They are acutely aware of their own mortality, and they readily associate past events: the time that a woman hung up her laundry one day and died in childbirth the next; the time that two expectant mothers shared the same hut and only one survived.

"Mine own dear love, —I no sooner conceived an hope that I should be made a mother by thee, but with it entered the consideration of a mother's duty, and shortly after followed the apprehension of danger," Elizabeth Joceline of Cambridgeshire, England, wrote to her unborn child in 1622. Joceline composed an entire book of advice and instruction to that child, to help it in the event of her own death, for in the early seventeenth century many women died in childbirth, and "widowers and stepmothers were common figures of life and lore," as one writer has put it. Today we might call Elizabeth Joceline prescient, but in her own time she was just a realist. She gave birth to a daughter but died of childbirth fever nine days later. Her book had gone through three editions by 1625.

VI

Birth and Hatching— Emergence

What I remember most about being pregnant is not the discomfort, not the forty extra pounds and the impossibly taut belly, but the interminable waiting as I went one, two, three weeks past my due date. I didn't know it at the time, but a bone spur

on my pelvis was preventing my already full-term fetus from dropping and preventing me from going into labor. In any other day and age, I wouldn't have survived this transition to reproducing adult; my daughter, if she had lived through such an ordeal, would probably have been raised by a stepmother, her copy of Elizabeth Joceline's book, or its equivalent, growing dog-eared with the years.

Not knowing anything about the bone spur or the cesarean that was to spare me from being culled by natural selection, feeling only vaguely that something might go wrong, was going wrong, I found those three hot, humid weeks in July most excruciating. They were a torment, I felt, custom-designed for me, who hates waiting any length of time, even five minutes in a checkout line. And this wasn't just waiting *for* something. It was waiting to *become* something. When the baby was born, I would be a mother; until then I was something in between, not just a child but not yet a parent. For those three weeks I was in a state of suspension much as drops of moisture were suspended in the thick July air. But, of course, I was much more thundercloud than drop.

The cloud did finally burst—thanks to my doctor, to modern medicine, and to a clean, well-equipped hospital—and I gave birth to a beautiful, healthy daughter weighing nine pounds and fifteen ounces. I thought the torment was over, but three years later, when my husband acquired four sheep from a neighbor who was retiring to Rhode Island, I came to realize that one of my fates in life would be to relive this torment time and time again. Of the four sheep he brought home that fine fall day, three, it became increasingly evident, were pregnant. Not that this worried me at first. Discounting my own experience, birth is a natural process, after all. An animal's survival depends on it going smoothly. But then I recollected that for centuries humans have bred sheep to give birth to twins and that twins always pose additional risks.

The only way a lamb fits easily through the ewe's pelvis is by presenting itself in a diving position: forelegs first. But lambs often try to come out backwards, sideways, at attention (with both forelegs at their sides), and saluting (with one foreleg raised). With two lambs,

I once figured, there is still only one easy presentation—both lambs in the diving position—but some 120 combinations of difficult ones, any and all of which might require assistance. And I had never even witnessed the birth of a puppy or a kitten, much less assisted with that of a large animal.

The deliveries of the first two ewes went so smoothly that I thought I might not need to try my hand at midwifery. Then one day I noticed that the third ewe had a mass the color and size of an orange hanging out her backside, a condition we identified as a prolapsed uterus. I called the vet, and he said to slide the errant tissue back inside and hold it there with a prolapse retainer, a piece of plastic that looks somewhat like a large tongue depressor with arms. The depressor part fits inside the ewe, and the arms are tied to strands of wool on either side of her. "But how will the lambs get out?" I remember asking. He responded that they would easily dislodge the retainer if they came out on their own, but that the chances of this were not good. We were told to keep a close eye on the ewe and assist her if necessary.

My husband and I arranged our schedules so that one of us was usually home (since we both were working at home at the time, this was easier than it sounds), and we took turns checking the ewe in the middle of the night, when the skies were dark and the air was sharp and cold. I never liked getting up and dressed to go outside on those January nights (my daughters, two of them by then, were still young enough to be getting us up several times a night as it was), but once outside I usually found that I stayed much longer than necessary. The heat the sheep gave off made it seem almost warm in the shed, where the only sounds were the munching of hay, the chewing of cud, the occasional owl hooting or dog barking. It was a time to reflect on life: on writing, raising children, and tending this small flock of sheep, a combination of activities that seemed to have little in common except that two of the three required fencing and all kept me up at night.

One day at last I noticed the ewe was behaving strangely. Snorting and breathing heavily, she pawed the ground. She lay down, only to get right up again. I checked our bible on sheep, *Raising Sheep the Modern Way* (how our library has expanded since the acquisition of these animals), and learned that those are the signs of labor, but the book also said that labor should progress in a matter of hours. This behavior went on all afternoon and into the night. Don't ask me what I was waiting for. Some sign, I suppose, that the ewe was in pain and needed help: a moan or a cry. Sometime close to midnight the absurdity of this hit me. I was waiting for the sheep to do something that she was unable to do, no matter how difficult her labor. For a human a cry brings others, helping hands that can lift fallen trees, pour water on fires, pull out babies. For a sheep, though, a sheep in the wild at least, a cry brings not assistance but wolves and coyotes. If this sheep was suffering, she would continue to do it in silence.

Suddenly I was mobilized. I ran to the house to rouse a friend who had offered to help, then fetched supplies—Vaseline, iodine, hot soapy water, and towels—and scrubbed my hands and arms. Within the hour, my friend and I had delivered two healthy lambs, one after the other. The wet, black creatures slid out onto the fresh hay, sneezed, bleated, and in five minutes were trying to stand on their long, well-developed legs.

It was the first time that I had ever seen a precocial animal being born, and I remember being both thrilled and a little shocked. I was used to newborns that could neither stand nor walk for almost a year, and here were these lambs, only ten minutes old, hopping about, poking their noses through the slats of their lambing pen. I was used to mothers who held their young to their breasts so that they could nurse, and here were these lambs searching about for their mother's teats, sucking on everything they came in contact with. I felt as if I had been allowed a glimpse at some strange new world. And it was a new world, an ovine world, a world where newborns are quick on their feet and where mothers mother without hands but with bleats and tongues and ovine body language. Eventually the ewe will only have to shift her hind leg and her lambs will be called in for supper.

If I ever thought, though, that these lambs were any less needy, any less requiring of their mother's attention than, for example, my own two daughters, I was very wrong. Lambs are precocial, it is true; their motor and sensory systems are well developed at birth, in tip-top operating condition, but they can no more survive on their own than a chicken can fly to the moon. Like all mammalian young, these lambs need milk from their mother's mammary glands in order to grow and maintain their body temperature, and to obtain this milk on a regular basis they need to stick with their mother, a particular problem for young that are so well coordinated at birth.

And if I ever thought of my daughters as playing little part in their own survival, I was also wrong. My daughters had behaviors and reflexes—rooting, clinging, sucking, crying, gazing behaviors—that were the equivalent of the teat-searching behaviors of the lambs. These were their ways of providing themselves with milk, warmth, dry diapers, closeness, comfort, all the things that human infants need to survive. Or rather, these were their ways of persuading my husband and me to provide them with those things. My daughters may have been slightly less proficient at survival than the lambs, but capable little things they were, not at all the passive receptacles of parental care I once took them for.

I wasn't the only one. Until quite recently most psychologists and biologists, not to mention most parents, have viewed newborns as helpless and vulnerable things, lumps of clay to be shaped by their parents, and "little more intelligent than a vegetable," as one professor of childhood diseases wrote in 1895. Newborns are unable to get around in the world, it is true, and they are unable to survive in the absence of a caring adult. But they are marvelously capable, as no grown person could be, of inspiring their parents to incredible acts of love and devotion: to midnight feedings and endless diaper changes, to daily rituals of patient caregiving.

Marsupials are perhaps the best example of just how wrongheaded the old infant-as-helpless-being, parent-as-provider-for-helpless-infant view of things is. Because marsupials lack a placenta and can only incubate their young inside for a short while (one to two weeks in most species), they give birth to undeveloped, embryoniclike things the size of bumblebees or navy beans. One might expect that the extreme immaturity of these young would call for increased care and solicitude on the part of their mothers. But just the opposite is true.

When a marsupial mother gives birth, she is oblivious to the fact. Her offspring—though naked, deaf, and blind, and with little more than buds where their hind limbs and tail will be—climb, without any help from their mother, up and out of her uterus, across her great expanse of belly, and into her pouch, where they attach themselves to a teat. There they remain, anchored to their food supply, until they have grown much larger and are covered with fur and ready to leave the pouch—a period of ten months for a marsupial like the gray kangaroo of Australia. The mother, meanwhile, may clean her pouch a little more often than usual, but otherwise she shows no maternal behavior. Even those marsupials that lack pouches, the arboreal opossums of South America, give no sign of being aware that they have given birth. Their young are born with well-developed forearms and grasping reflexes, essential features in infants that spend their early months hanging on to oblivious mothers.

Other newborns have other adaptations that reveal them to be not so much helpless as perfectly adapted to the environment in which they find themselves. The cuckoo, a stranger to the nest in which its mother has left her egg, hatches as a blind, featherless chick that must be fed and kept clean and warm by its adoptive parents. Yet at hatching it is perfectly capable of maneuvering each of the eggs containing its foster siblings onto its back, then climbing backwards up the side of the nest and heaving those eggs overboard. Dolphin young, born under water, know enough to swim immediately to the surface to get air. Infant elephant seals are not licked and dried by their mothers at birth (probably because elephant seals have so few predators), but instead flip sand onto their own backs to absorb the birth fluids and keep themselves warm. Bat babies, delivered while their mothers hang from the roofs of caves, have no time to learn the knack of living upside down. They are born with well-developed claws on their toes, grappling hooks that allow them to cling to their mothers' fur. And just to ensure that there isn't a mishap, a moment when the slippery newborn might fall to the ground, where it would be devoured by the beetles living in the thick carpet of guano there, the young are born feet—i.e., grappling hooks—first, a presentation unique among mammals. Within hours bat pups are able to hang by themselves from the cave ceiling while their mothers leave the colony to feed.

Far from being helpless, then, the young have sophisticated resources and behaviors that allow them to establish a toehold in the world in which they find themselves: a nest inside a wooden box for the bluebird nestling; on the hoof for the lamb; in a crib in a nursery for the twentieth-century American baby. Yet, as we know, they cannot go it alone. Every newborn in every species which takes care of its young after birth must have a parent out there, a parent to listen and respond to its cries of hunger, a parent to sense its first tentative rooting for a teat, a parent to gaze back into its eyes, a parent to pick the lice off of it or protect it from predators. The dolphin infant knows enough to go to the surface for air, but before it can do this, its mother must break the umbilical cord by whirling around sharply to face the infant immediately after it is born. It is not parent providing care to helpless young but parent and young, together, performing carefully synchronized, ruthlessly selected dances of reproduction and survival. The newborn is born knowing its steps, but, like all ballroom dancers, it must have a partner. The parent may be a capable dancer, but it certainly helps if the signals the newborn sends are strong and clear.

It also helps if the parent is paying attention to those signals, so many females isolate themselves at the time of birth. Some become uncommonly aggressive, even toward members of their own species. This aggressiveness helps to protect them, of course, during this period when they are less mobile than usual and their young are easy prey, but it also gives them the time and the space to focus on this important event. It allows them to smell a newborn's smell and listen to a newborn's cry, to taste a newborn's taste and memorize a newborn's shape. Isolation increases the probability that parent and child will actually interact with each other at birth.

The birth process—itself, the contractions and release of fluids, the smells and sensations—also increases this probability by focusing a mother's attention on her body and, especially, on that part of her body where the young will emerge. In many mammals, an increase in self-grooming is a sign that birth is imminent. This simple act seems to smooth the transition that each new mother must make: from self-absorbed being to a being absorbed in some other, from aggressive carnivore to caring mother, from wanderer to nurturing nester. For solitary animals, which most mammals are, birth is an extraordinary moment. It is the beginning of the longest relationship they will experience in their adult lifetimes, the only relationship, other than a brief encounter with a male of their species.

Unlike most mammals, sheep do not lick or groom themselves before giving birth, but they have another way of making sure their attention is focused on their lambs. Sheep would normally be repulsed by the smell and taste of amniotic fluids. Ewes that have just given birth, though, find these fluids extremely delicious, and they lick their lambs vigorously so as to imbibe every drop. At the same time, of course, they are drying their lambs and stimulating breathing and other bodily functions. They are also getting to know their lambs' smell and sounds and making the transition to motherhood.

All these behaviors surrounding birth—an increase in aggression or self-grooming, a pursuit of solitude, a short, intense love of amniotic fluids—are brought about, of course, by hormonal changes. The precise hormonal changes associated with pregnancy, birth, egg laying, and incubation are different for different species, but they all serve the same purpose: to carefully orchestrate the events of gestation, egg laying, nest building, and/or milk production. In many animals, the hormones of pregnancy and birth are not necessary to produce parental feelings (as any adoptive parent knows), but they are necessary to coordinate birth, milk supply, and parental involvement, a synchronization that has been necessary for the survival of most animals for most of time.

As soon as birth or hatching takes place, though, hormones by themselves cease to be sufficient to maintain parental behavior. The young then take over as the most important stimulus acting on their parents. If a mother rat has her ovaries, adrenal glands, and pituitary glands removed, her mothering behavior, other than nursing, is unaffected. If, however, her pups are removed at birth, all her mothering behavior will disappear within four days.

This makes sense. There must be feedback, otherwise the mother whose litter dies or is eaten will continue to lactate and build nests and search for her young. She will waste valuable time and energy that she could be spending on a second litter. Parents are primed for parental behavior by their hormones and the act of birth, but in order for their behavior to continue, they must have partners that are responding appropriately. A primate mother will carry a dead infant around for several days, holding it and grooming it. Beluga mothers that have lost their calves have been seen swimming with planks of wood. But as the plank of wood or dead infant fails to respond to the mother, the behaviors fade.

The ewe-lamb dance, the bluebird-nestling dance are just two possibilities. Each species has its own two-step, each enabling its young to survive in a specific ecological niche. For white-tailed deer, the dance begins in much the same way as for sheep, with the birth of one or two fawns, which the mother licks clean and which are able to stand and nurse within the hour. But almost immediately one starts to see variations. Unlike sheep, but like other animals that remain in the same place after birth, the doe quickly consumes the placenta and the fetal membranes, for these bloody tissues might give her and her young away. Then, as another precaution against predators, the young fawns bed down on their own soon after nursing. They do not stick by their mother as lambs do but choose their own bedding site, untainted by the strong scent of their mother. Each fawn beds down separately, and even at night the mother sleeps apart, in a bed or scrape some thirty feet away from her young. Whereas a lamb nurses ten to forty times a day, a fawn nurses only two or three times. When a doe is ready to feed her offspring, she searches for them with her neck outstretched, using her acute sense of smell. She begins looking near the spot where they last nursed, and if she can't find them with her nose, she may call to them with a soft, plaintive mew.

My daughters came across one of these bedded-down fawns in the woods behind our house, and it was so motionless that they thought at first they had found a fur hat that someone had dropped, a beautiful, chestnut-colored hat with white spots. Then the hat blinked. They didn't think the fawn had been abandoned—it was far too clean and too quiet—but they did work themselves into a frenzy imagining what the fawn's father, the stag, would do to them if he found them there. They left in such a panic that my older daughter, seven at the time, ran right into our neighbor's electric fence. If only they had known, oh, daughters of mine, about the indifference of that stag and the solitary road of most mammalian mothers.

The arboreal and social existence of primates has led to some interesting permutations of the mother-infant dance. Most primates that are active during the day give birth during the night. Birth is not timed to isolate the female, as in solitary animals, but to coincide with the group's activities. A female who stops foraging to deliver an infant risks being left behind by the rest of her group. But a female who delivers when the other group members are resting in nearby trees is protected by their presence. The diurnal squirrel monkey always begins labor between dusk and dawn, and if delivery hasn't taken place by morning, labor will stop and begin again the next evening. Humans still have evidence of this adaptive timing. A human birth is much more likely to occur at night or in the early morning and much less likely to occur during the day.

In the treetops, where many primate females give birth, newborns also run the risk of falling during delivery. Most primates, therefore, assist in their own deliveries by pulling their young out, holding and licking their infant's head as it emerges. Most primate young, for their part, are extremely active at birth. In several squirrel monkey births that have been observed, the infant, as soon as its shoulders were freed, grabbed hold of the fur on its mother's belly and helped to pull itself from the womb. Within minutes it was crawling around on its mother searching for her teats. Most primate infants are strong enough and coordinated enough to cling to their mothers unaided after birth (even as their mothers swing through the trees), but some of the higher primates have poor motor control at birth. Chimpanzee and gorilla infants must be supported by their mothers for the first few weeks of life.

Like the doe, most primates also consume the afterbirth when it is delivered. Chimpanzees eat it with wads of leaves, as they do their animal prey, and it probably provides them with nutrients in addition to removing smells that may attract predators.[1]

The hatching of a bird, it is often said, is not so dramatic an event as the birth of a mammal. But then again, those that feel this way are mammals, and perhaps they would naturally give the fetus's forced expulsion from its cushioned, seagoing world more points for dramatic interest than the chick's escape from its calcium carbonate prison. In any event, the bird's transition to life on the outside is more gradual than that of the fetus. Chicks begin to breathe several days before hatching (as soon as their beaks reach the air pocket at the tip of the egg), and they are exposed to sounds, and maybe even sights, while still in their shells. The fetus, by contrast, is shut off from almost all sensory input until it emerges from the womb. One moment the fetus is totally dependent on the maternal circulatory system for oxygen, food, and waste removal; the next, it is an independent being that must breathe, eat, and excrete for itself in a sensory bouillabaisse of totally new sights, sounds, and sensations.

But hatching is probably harder work than birth (at least for the young). For one thing, the shell has been designed to withstand the weight of the parents. For another, the chick must labor in an extremely confined space with only two tools: an egg tooth (the horny shield that covers its still soft bill) and a pair of hatching muscles. These are hard muscles that extend down the neck and that atrophy shortly after hatching. The chick begins its escape by jabbing its egg tooth repeatedly against the shell. When it finally makes its first puncture, a starlike hole rimmed with cracks, it turns its body within the shell and begins working on a second puncture, then a third. When it has made a circle of these punctures, it contracts its hatching muscles and presses against the shell. With a final series of kicks and pushes, it forces the shell apart and topples out, exhausted.

The process can take hours or days, depending on the species, but it is usually over sometime in the morning, perhaps because this gives the young time to be fed before nightfall. Parents don't usually help their young in their labors, but some may pick at the edge of the gap that the chick has made. The ostrich has been known to crack its extremely hard shell with its breastbone, then seize the chick with its foot and pull it out. Most parents, though, do no more than stand over their eggs and urge their young on with low, encouraging notes. Since the offspring of precocial birds leave the nest shortly after hatching, it is important that all the chicks in a clutch hatch at once, a synchrony that they achieve by talking to one another, and to their parent, before hatching takes place. Bobwhite chicks, twelve to sixteen in a nest, start communicating about twenty-four hours before hatching with a rhythmic clicking that encourages some chicks to work faster, much as singing helps an army platoon stay in step.

❧

If every animal has these species-specific behaviors at birth or hatching, these ways that parent and offspring interact to ensure that the young have a good chance of survival, what about humans? What behaviors of the human female are the equivalents of the ewe's rapid licking of her lamb, the dolphin mother's quick twirl to break the umbilical cord? What behaviors of the human infant are the equivalents of the bobwhite chick's clicking, the newborn fawn's camouflaged stillness? Do humans and their newborns, too, have certain predictable ways of interacting at birth?

John Bowlby, an English psychologist, began to look at human birth from the viewpoint of adaptation and biology in the 1950s and was one of the first to ask the all-important question What are the behaviors of the newborn infant, fresh from its mother's womb, for? Why is the newborn able to cling so strongly that it can support its own weight? Why does a newborn tend to orient toward a high-pitched, female voice, to follow the human face with its eyes, to cry but to be quieted when held in a human's arms?

It seems incredible to think that no one had asked these questions before, but, as I've said already, newborns had long been thought of as little more than lumps of clay, blank slates to be inscribed by their parents, learning machines awaiting instructions. Freud had described the attachment and great love that come to exist between most mothers and their children, and had attributed them to the fact that mothers feed their infants. The infant associates the breast with the pleasant sensation of being fed, Freud proposed, and later on it begins to associate the breast with its mother. Behaviorists, too, thought that a child's behavior, including its attachment to its mother, resulted from a series of learned responses.

Bowlby's interest in newborns and in the relationship of mother and child came not from his observations of babies but rather from his observations of maladjusted children. When Bowlby worked in a school for disturbed children and, later, in England's National Health Service, he saw many adolescents who were completely withdrawn and lacking in emotion. His colleagues at the time believed that these children's problems stemmed entirely from the workings of their own minds, from conflicts between their aggressive and libidinal drives and from fantasies that these conflicts generated. But Bowlby could not help noticing that the children all had one thing in common: They all lacked stable relationships with their mothers.

Bowlby could not find anything in the psychological literature that helped him understand what had happened to these children. When he was searching, though, he happened upon a translation of a paper by the European biologist Konrad Lorenz on imprinting in geese: the process by which newly hatched goslings recognize and become attached to their parents. Bowlby was immediately impressed by Lorenz's descriptions of a gosling's distress if it came to be separated from its parent, for he found the gosling's reaction strikingly similar to the separation anxiety of a toddler who is parted from its mother. He was also struck by the fact that this strong bond in geese is formed on the basis of something other than oral gratification. Geese parents do not feed their precocial young, remember, they only guide them to the place where they will find food.

Lorenz's work on imprinting in geese somehow allowed Bowlby to see through the veils of Freudianism and behaviorism to a fundamental human truth. The need to form an attachment to a caregiver is as instinctive in human infants, Bowlby proposed, as it is in geese and many other animals. And the behaviors of infants have been shaped by natural selection to bring this attachment about. The infant's cry, he said, is designed to get its mother's attention and bring her into close proximity; its gaze, its innate ability to follow the human face with its eyes, is designed to keep her there.

Bowlby called these actions attachment behaviors, and he argued that attachment arose in the course of the evolution of many species as a way of providing infants with the protection they needed to survive. Along the way attachment became a need itself, every bit as important as protection, food, or warmth. In humans it is the need to develop a sustaining, stable relationship with another human being. It was this relationship, the foundation for all other relationships in a human being's life, that was missing from the lives of those troubled adolescents.

Attachment, in this view, is not a by-product of the gratification of hunger, as Freudians and behaviorists had argued. Rather attachment comes first, and through it an infant ensures that its needs are met. It was with this insight that Bowlby revolutionized the practice of psychiatry and psychology, making sense of the behavior of newborns and giving the relationship between parent and child a critical role in a child's developmental equation. It was, of course, a role that poets, mothers, people everywhere with an ounce of common sense had always recognized. Bowlby, as we will see later, made the mistake of overemphasizing protection and underemphasizing food and the other needs of infants. But this mistake is understandable given that he was trying to make a clean break with Freud and Freud's insistence on the primary role feeding plays in the development of affection. Fortunately this error did not get in the way of the profound importance of his ideas.

Since Bowlby presented his attachment theory, researchers have found ample evidence to support the idea that the human infant is far from passive at birth, that it comes into the world with a whole repertoire of behaviors to encourage its parents and to force them into a relationship in which they will be willing to provide it with the long-term care it needs, care that the parents, in turn, have been selected to provide. Studies of the infant's cry have found that it is akin to an ambulance siren in terms of its spectrographic properties and its ability to arouse immediate displeasure and alarm. Men and women experience many of the same physiological changes in response to an infant's cry—intense anxiety coupled with changes in blood pressure and heart rate—but in lactating women the infant's cry also elevates breast temperature and produces a letdown reflex. The infant thereby assures itself of getting food as well as comfort and warmth.

Since crying would expose an infant to predation, it may seem odd that infants have evolved this way of getting their parents' attention, but few evolutionary mechanisms are without some compromise: in this case, the danger of attracting predators versus the probability that an infant separated from its parents and unable to let them know its whereabouts would die anyway. Also, crying, in the environment in which humans evolved, may have been a method of last resort. Since babies stayed with their mothers most of the time, they would rarely have needed to cry. Those mothers who left their babies, causing them to begin crying, would have been selected against because of the increased risk of predation and, perhaps, of abuse. There are few sounds that humans find as unnerving as an infant's cry, and child abuse often begins with a parent trying to stop a baby from crying.

While an infant's cry summons its parents, its gaze and, later on, its smile reward them for their care. Few parents fail to comment on their infants' eyes at birth, and the ability to make eye contact is one of the most unusual things about the human newborn. Eye contact is relatively unimportant in other primates, and researchers have proposed that it has replaced the infant monkey's grasp, its ability to cling at birth. The monkey infant holds its mother with its strong fingers; the human infant, with its eyes. At birth human infants focus best on objects approximately twelve inches away (the distance to a mother's eyes as an infant breast-feeds), and even when they are as little as ten minutes old, they would rather look at a human face than at anything else in the world. The human face is the stimulus that best sets off firing in the neurons of the infant's brain.

If infants have evolved to bring about attachments, what about mothers? How do human mothers behave at birth? Bowlby did not address this question, perhaps because mothers in England in the 1950s and '60s were usually so heavily anesthetized during delivery that they hardly behaved at all. Moreover, hospitals tended to separate mothers from their infants soon after birth in order to prevent the spread of infectious diseases. No, the question of what human females do at birth had to wait until females could be observed under somewhat natural settings. Until the procedures in maternity wards were changed, as they were in the 1970s, largely due to two pediatricians: Marshall Klaus and John Kennell.

Like Bowlby, Klaus and Kennell did not start out to study mother-infant interactions at birth; they arrived at that point from their observations of older babies and their parents, and their sometimes abusive relationships. As they explain it in the first edition (1976) of their book *Maternal-Infant Bonding,* "An important impetus to studying the mother-infant bond occurred ten to fifteen years ago when the staffs of intensive care nurseries observed that after heroic measures had been used to save prematures, those infants would sometimes return to emergency rooms battered and almost destroyed by their parents, even though the infants had been sent home intact and thriving."

Like Bowlby, Klaus and Kennell were also impressed by animal behavior studies: in particular, studies of maternal behavior in sheep and goats that showed there to be a critical period after birth when the ewe or the dam had to be with her young in order to form an attachment to them. If the young were removed during this period, the mother rejected them instead. Might a similar phenomenon be happening in humans? Klaus and Kennell wondered. Might the fact that the mothers of these premature infants were unable to be with their children after birth be the cause of the future abuse? And if this time together was important for premature infants and their mothers, must it not be important for full-term infants and their mothers as well?

The first hour after birth, the two doctors proposed, is the human sensitive period. This is the time, they said, when mothers are most receptive to stimuli from their infants, the time when mothers are most likely to bond to their children. Whether a mother and infant have this time together can have long-lasting consequences. This hour, they went on to assert, will significantly affect the quality of the mother's future attachment to her child.

It was a dramatic proposal, and it had immediate, dramatic results. Parents demanded to be with their infants in the hour after birth, and hospital practices came to be totally revamped: fathers were allowed in the delivery room to be part of the bonding process; medications during delivery were cut down; special birthing rooms were built.

It was Klaus and Kennell's ideas that led to the changes that allowed me to be awake during my two cesarean sections, their ideas that enabled my husband to be present and that gave us both those indelible glimpses of our daughters as they took their first breaths and screamed their first, purple screams. And surely hospital practices needed to be changed and birth needed to be viewed more as a normal, healthy experience and less as the culmination of a nine-month illness. So I feel I should be kind to Klaus and Kennell but I can't be. Their bonding doctrine, their insistence that early postpartum contact is necessary for good attachment, may have helped me, but it hurt so many others, women who had to be separated from their infants at birth and then carried with them the guilt that, because of this separation, their entire relationships with their children were in jeopardy. And for what?

Though bonding theory was accepted with enthusiasm by expectant parents and a number of studies soon published seemed to back the theory, these studies were later shown to be seriously flawed in their methodology (either they failed to use double-blind tests or they could not be replicated). Most careful, scientific studies have found that early contact has no lasting effect on the quality of a mother's relationship with her child.

Confounded by the rapidity and breadth of the changes that bonding theory brought about and the thinness of the evidence upon which the theory stood, one critic of bonding theory has asked "how and why such flawed science has become so scientifically acceptable." His answer is that bonding theory gave hospitals a supposedly scientific basis for change. The practice of separating mothers and infants developed out of real concerns about introducing infectious diseases into the nursery, and simply abandoning this practice in response to parents' demands for more contact with their infants (demands that increased as infant mortality rates declined) was impossible from an obstetrical point of view. With Klaus and Kennell's bonding theory, though, and the studies that seemed to back it up, obstetricians could claim that the benefits of increased contact outweighed the risks.

But if we've learned anything at all about diversity of behavior in the animal world and about how animals have adapted to their different ecological niches, we shouldn't be too surprised that studies haven't supported bonding theory. Klaus and Kennell used sheep and goats to illuminate the behavior of humans, overlooking the vast differences between these species.[2] Sheep and goats, herd animals, must form rapid, exclusive bonds with their young because they will be on the move within hours and mothers must somehow maintain contact with their newborns. Kids and lambs must stick by their mothers. These bonds are also necessary because all the females in a herd of sheep and goats give birth at about the same time. Reproduction is synchronized so that births occur when the conditions are most favorable for lactating mothers and/or newly weaned young, but synchronization also creates many opportunities for mix-ups. Humans, by contrast, can give birth at any time of the year. They also carry their young. Since mix-ups are much less of a problem, humans don't have the same need for rapid, exclusive bonds.

What Klaus and Kennell were overlooking the most, though, as they leapt from sheep and goats to humans, was the human female's experience with birth, an experience very different from that of other animal females and one that has itself selected against the formation of rapid bonds.

The human female's great difficulty in giving birth is not a Western invention, as some might think. It is truly the Curse of Eve, the birthright of all women, guaranteed by *Homo sapiens'* big brain and upright stance. Walking on two legs necessitates that humans have a narrow, rigid pelvis (one that can bear more than half the weight of the skeleton), but a narrow, rigid pelvis makes the delivery of infants difficult, especially infants with large brains. As the ancestors of *Homo sapiens* began to walk on two legs (perhaps in response to changes in their climate and habitat) and then to evolve bigger and bigger brains, great pressures were brought to bear on the most fundamental constraint of mammalian birth: the ability of the embryo to make its way through its mother's pelvic opening.

Bigger brains gave their hominid owners great advantages in adapting to new environments and in forming long-term alliances with their mates and other hominids, but they also precipitated an obstetric crisis that resulted in the human infant being born at an earlier and earlier stage of its development. "Over time," as one anthropologist explains, "many [women] must have died in childbirth; but a few, by genetic chance, bore their young earlier—delivering more immature babies that easily slipped through the birth canal. These females and their babies survived more often, passing the critical trait to bear highly immature infants across the eons to women around the world today."

During this time, women also began to benefit from assistance during birth. Ape mothers can pull their infants out themselves, but the hominid female's pelvis and the tight fit of the infant's head necessitated an entirely new set of rotations for the infant as it made its way through the birth canal and a new orientation of the infant's head and shoulders. If the hominid female tried to assist in her own delivery, she would be pulling against the normal flexion of the infant's body and would risk doing serious damage, particularly to the nerves of the neck.

Scientists call the infants that human beings give birth to "exterogestate fetuses," fetuses that develop outside the uterus, and they estimate that they would need to spend another six months in utero to be as advanced as great ape infants at birth with regard to motor skills and brain development. Like all primates, human infants have many features of a precocial animal—they are born with their eyes open, and they are able to hear and smell at birth, but for nine months or longer they must be carried everywhere they go.

All of this had profound effects on the female at the moment of birth. These premature infants demanded, of course, increased amounts of care, which human mothers, with their arms freed by their upright stance, were better able to provide. Even with a premature delivery, birth was still difficult, and many mothers and their infants did not survive it. Those mothers who bonded immediately to their infants and grieved long and hard at their deaths might not reproduce again for a long time. Those infants who became instantly attached to their mothers, to the sound of their voices and the smell of their breasts, would suffer if their mothers died and they had to be given to another family.

In humans, in other words, the species with the most difficulty giving birth *and* the greatest capacity for love and long-lasting relationships, a rapid, exclusive attachment would be anything but adaptive. Human mothers or their substitutes—their mates, mothers, midwives, or doctors—must provide some care for infants shortly after birth. In that way the first hour is and always will be a critical period, but bonding, that sense of deep attachment, does not necessarily take place then. It takes time to develop, both because the ecology of humans gives us that time and because factors in our evolution have selected against rapid attachment. "Love for the baby comes gradually," Dr. Benjamin Spock told parents in his best-selling book on parenting, *Baby Care.* This is what most psychologists thought before the bonding craze hit, and this is what they think now.

This loose time frame for human attachment might well explain some of the more curious things about infants and their mothers observed around the world: the widespread custom of not naming infants at birth; the indifference of many women when they first see their babies; the fact that neonates are commonly viewed as ugly; even why infants do not smile for the first two months.

Biologists have long puzzled over the timing of the infant's social smile, wondering why it would take so long for this behavior, the most powerful reinforcer of maternal behavior, to emerge. Some see its late emergence as more evidence that our species is secondarily altricial; in this view the delayed smile results from infants' prematurity at birth. More recently it has been suggested that the timing of the infant's social smile may have come about initially as a result of human infants being born more and more prematurely, but that it has been maintained because of the advantage it offers to a species with such a high rate of infant mortality.

"The strong feelings of attraction that many parents describe in response to the social smile at three months may be timed appropriately with the end of a period of fairly high infant mortality," the pediatrician and author Melvin Konner has suggested. "A three-month-old has passed a critical period for survival and parents can then afford the heavy emotional investment, the attachment that other animals make at birth."

Today, in those parts of the world where infant and maternal mortality have fallen greatly and mothers now expect a healthy, happy outcome to their pregnancies, women are eager to become attached at birth. They feel guilty if they are anything less than infatuated with their infants and work hard to overcome feelings of indifference. Yet for most of human existence, an attachment that started small and grew over time was also part of our birthright, as much a part as difficult labor, midwives, and our curiously immature infants.

❧

Given this loose attachment, though, what do human mothers do in the time immediately following delivery? Do they, like other mammalian mothers, have a series of stereotypical behaviors? Or is their behavior determined more by culture than by biology and by such idiosyncratic factors as whether or not the baby is planned, the mother's relationship with the infant's father, her past experiences with children and her experiences as a child herself?

In addition to their "maternal sensitive period," Klaus and Kennell also claimed that human mothers interact with their infants in a characteristic way. "An orderly and predictable pattern of behavior was observed when each mother of the full-term infants first saw her infant," they wrote in one of their earliest papers on bonding. "Commencing hesitantly with fingertip contact on the extremities, within four to five minutes she began caressing the trunk with her palm, simultaneously showing progressively heightened excitement, which continued for several minutes. Her activity then often diminished, sometimes to such a degree that she fell asleep with the infant at her side."

Subsequent researchers have not found anything like the uniformity that Klaus and Kennell described, but they have observed that certain behaviors are very common in the first hour after birth: the making of eye contact with the infant (except in cultures where eye contact is discouraged, the Maya of the Yucatán Peninsula, for example), high-pitched vocalizations and cooing, touching and rubbing of the infant with the hand and fingertips, initiation of breast feeding, and holding the infant on the left side.

Lee Salk was one of the first to note that mothers tend to hold their infants much more often on their left side than on their right, a behavior he attributed to the soothing effect of the maternal heartbeat, which had, after all, been an important feature of the infant's intrauterine life. Since Salk's original observation in 1960, the left-lateral preference has been confirmed by several studies, and close to 80 percent of all women, left-handed and right-handed, it seems, hold their babies on their left sides more often than on their right. More recently it has been found that infants have an innate preference for turning their heads to the right, a preference which may have shaped their mothers' holding patterns and, indeed, their handedness, since mothers holding their infants on their left side have their right hands free.

Or perhaps it was the mothers' handedness that shaped the infants' head turning. In any case, in Wenda Trevathan's study of one hundred mothers who gave birth at the Birth Center in El Paso, the seventy-one mothers who immediately pulled their infants to their left side were able to initiate breast feeding approximately thirteen minutes earlier than were those who held their babies on the right. Another researcher has found that those mothers who do not hold their infants on their left (more often than on their right) are more likely to have had problems during their pregnancy or emotional problems before pregnancy. Some now think that a failure to hold an infant on the left side reflects a mother's early insensitivity to her infant's needs.

Another thing that human females often do at birth harkens back to the question of paternal certainty, which plagues all animals that fertilize their eggs internally. And it harkens back to the human female's great need for a mate who will stand by her and help her to raise her young. Maternal certainty is always assured at the moment of birth, of course, but paternal certainty is not, and women who have just delivered often comment on how much the infant resembles its father or members of the father's family—in the eyes, the hair, the shape of the ears, head, or even the feet. In conversations immediately after birth, paternal resemblance is discussed much more often than maternal resemblance, studies have found, and in almost every case it is the mother who remarks on the resemblance. I don't recall having said anything of the kind to my husband when either of our daughters was born, but then again, when they emerged, the spitting image of my husband, anything I said would have been redundant.

Whose Child
Is This?

I t is June in Texas, in a large cave north of San Antonio where twenty million free-tailed bats, give or take a hundred thousand or so, have begun arriving from the south to give birth. This cave is their maternity center, their birthing room, and, pregnant, they have flown eight hundred miles from their wintering grounds in central Mexico to reach it, timing their arrival and the birth of their single pups to coincide with the explosion of moths in Texas in

June. Here, these tiny mammals, weighing just half an ounce, will be able to find food enough to carry them through the demanding period of lactation. Each night, each bat will eat about half its body weight in moths; the entire colony will consume about 150 tons.

Inside the cave, it should be cool, but twenty million creatures, even twenty million tiny creatures and their droppings, add up, and it is about one hundred humid degrees Fahrenheit. Even though it is daytime and bats are nocturnal, there is a constant swirl in the air and a constant din. One can pick out the high-pitched cries of adults as they circle the cave and the squeals, higher-pitched still, of newborns in their nursery, those areas in the cave where the mothers deposit their pups soon after giving birth. They fly them there crosswise on their bodies, with the pups' mouths grasping one teat and their hind legs tucked into the opposite armpit. Then the mothers go off to roost in another part of the cave. They will return only to nurse and only twice a day, once in the afternoon before leaving the cave for the night and once in the morning when they return.

For as long as human beings have wondered about things such as parental care and the evolution of animal behavior, these bats have been a puzzle. How does the bat mother find her pup again after she leaves it in the crowded nursery? How, among the thousands upon thousands of pink, furless, squealing bodies, does she pick out *her* pink, furless, squealing body? Or does she?

Perhaps she just nurses the first hungry pup that grabs hold of her teat. If every mother nursed just as indiscriminately, wouldn't the strongest, most vocal, most aggressive bat pups survive? Wouldn't the bat population as a whole benefit?

For many years, this was the way bat colonies were thought to work, and in books on animal behavior one can still read that bat mothers "returning to the cave nurse any baby." Similarly, it was once assumed that colonial seabirds, like common murres, that incubate their eggs cheek by jowl on sea cliffs do not necessarily incubate their own eggs or feed their own chicks. "As long as each bird succeeds in finding an egg to cover on its return home," wrote Chester A. Reed, an egg collector of the last century, "it is doubtful if the bird either knows, or cares, whether it is its own or not."

And, indeed, who could even imagine the alternative: that bat mothers could actually find and feed their own young in groups so dense they make a rush-hour train on the IRT line look like a private conveyance (one researcher counted five thousand free-tailed bats on a single square yard of cave wall), or that murres can locate their eggs, their chicks, on a rock dotted with similar eggs and chicks?

Then in the 1960s and '70s, scientists began to put this idea that evolution is a cooperative venture, in which each member of a species acts in such a way that the species as a whole grows fitter, to the test. The British biologist John Maynard Smith used computer simulations to show that group selection is not an evolutionarily stable strategy. It wouldn't last in the real world for the very pragmatic reason that it would soon be undermined by cheaters: by bat mothers that left their pups for others to nurse, by murres that let others incubate their eggs.

If nursing really were indiscriminate, natural selection should favor the female that placed her pup in the nursery for others to nurse and then shirked all nursing duties herself, as Gary McCracken and Mary Gustin, two biologists who have spent many summers studying the maternal behavior of bats, explain. "The female would save herself the substantial energy of milk production and, at the same time, would not jeopardize her own pup's survival any more than that of any other pup in the population."

The female would also keep herself in tip-top form for reproduction and would soon outprogeny the more conscientious females. Her cheating genes would spread but only until there were so many cheaters that cheating was no longer a viable strategy. Then, in a world overrun by cheaters, the best strategy for raising young would be for each parent to look after her own young, for each bat mother to nurse her own pup, each murre to incubate its own egg. Those young that were assured of receiving the care of their parents would be more likely to survive and reproduce, to pass on those caregiving genes and behavior that would lead this time to a strategy that can last generation after generation, millennium after millennium: a stable evolutionary strategy.

Sure enough, when biologists began to look closely at the parental behavior of bats and murres, they found exactly what Maynard Smith had predicted on the basis of his computer simulations. Common murres do incubate their own eggs, and they are very capable of identifying those eggs, using the eggs' distinctive background color and markings. And they feed their own chicks and learn the calls of those chicks before they have even hatched.

For some years, biologists continued to think that free-tailed bats parented in a group selectionist way. Then in the 1980s, in the bat caves of Texas, McCracken and Gustin tested theories of indiscriminate nursing by picking pairs of nursing pups and mothers off the cave walls and analyzing the relationship of each pair using blood and muscle tissue samples. The results of their tests were unequivocal. In 160 out of 167 pairs, females had found and were nursing their own pups. In only 7 pairs were mothers nursing pups that were not their own.

The researchers would have liked to learn more about the circumstances under which mothers nurse strange pups by marking pups at birth, then observing nursing pairs over time, but this kind of experiment was impossible to do because of the size of the bats' colony, the bats' sensitivity to light, and the unpredictability of when any one female will return to nurse. They had to settle for using an infrared video system to observe the bats' behavior.

Nonparental nursing occurs, the videos clearly showed, when pups steal milk from females that are searching for their own young. When a female lands in the nursery, she is aggressively pursued by every pup she meets. She guards her teats with folded wings and tries to shake off would-be milk thieves (whose ranks even include other mothers) by biting them and scratching them with her hind feet. But every so often, the videos showed, one of the thieves is successful.

Bat mothers no more choose to suckle each other's young, it seems, than Maine lobstermen tend each other's pots, as one biologist has put it. Some of us may recoil at this seemingly selfish strategy, but, remember, it is this strategy that has given us the world we know today. The complicated, enduring, real world, not some two-dimensional, fantasy world like that in a Walt Disney film. In this real world, infants that receive care usually receive it from their parents. Parents have a solid, genetic interest in their young; plus, they usually make the best caregivers. Because of their genetic similarities, they are most attuned to their young in small, important ways. This is not to say that adoption or care of young by animals other than parents never takes place. It does, as we will see, but usually in well-defined circumstances.

In order to provide care for their young, and their young only, parents must have a way of being able to pick them out, in a herd, a cave, a cliff face, or wherever else they happen to be bringing up baby. Ewes recognize their lambs by a combination of olfactory, visual, and auditory stimuli—by their smell, first of all, their look, and the sound of their bleat. Common murres use visual stimuli to recognize the patterns of their eggs and auditory stimuli for their chicks. But how does a bat mother find her pup in a nursery of five thousand or more pups?

When a female lands in the nursery, McCracken and Gustin's videos showed, she calls for several seconds, then begins crawling over and through the mass of pups. After moving about an inch or two, she stops, calls again, then continues. Her search usually ends when she shows interest in a particular pup, touching noses with it, smelling it, and exchanging cries, but sometimes she is so harassed by milk thieves that she gives up and flies away, presumably to try again later. A bat mother may screen eighteen hundred pups before she finds her own, the videos showed, but by returning to the place where she last nursed, she avoids screening the entire nursery. Bat pups painted with fluorescent spots were shown to move only a short distance between nursings, eighteen inches on the average.

McCracken and Gustin were not surprised that the bat mothers used vocalizations to locate their pups. Bats, after all, have an acute sense of hearing, and studies in other bat species had shown that mothers and their young communicate vocally and recognize each other's calls. When the two scientists used acoustical instruments to analyze the calls of more than three hundred free-tailed bat pups, they found that all calls were different in terms of duration, time between calls, maximum frequency, and the amount of sound energy at different frequencies. Though they all sound alike to the human ear, a "mother bat, with more sensitivity than these electronic instruments," the researchers concluded, "would probably have little difficulty recognizing the call of her own pup."

What did surprise McCracken and Gustin was that smell seems to be so important in the identification process, so they devised tests to see whether female bats could indeed discriminate between pups on the basis of smell alone. They picked nursing pairs off the cave wall and collected odors from the pups by rubbing them with clean cotton swabs. Mothers were then allowed to choose between a swab from the pup they had just been nursing and a swab from some other pup. In almost every case, mothers moved quickly to the swab from the pup they had nursed, sometimes placing their wings over it as if to suckle.

❦

Recognition, then, is the key that turns the lock of parental care in bats, as it has long been known to be the key to care in sheep and goats. Even during the years when the theory of group selectionism held sway, there were those who knew how difficult it is for a lamb or a young goat other than a parent's own to enter the exclusive club of parental affection. Shepherds and goatherds with an orphan lamb or kid on their hands had used every trick they could think of to fool another mother into believing the orphan was her own. Skinning the mother's own dead lamb and draping the skin over the orphan is the one that is best known, but squirting the orphan with kerosene or the mother's milk is said to work better.

Scientists can hardly be blamed, though, for taking so long to realize that the exclusivity of sheep and goats applies to all animals. For a while there appeared to be so many exceptions to the rule that parents care for their own young that recognition and exclusivity did not seem to be rules at all. There were the murres and the free-tailed bats, of course, as well as reports of adoption among many animals. Then there was the fact that the young of many species can be transferred from one nest into another with total acceptance by the parents. If the nestlings of altricial birds are moved into the nest of unrelated adults, the new adults will feed them as if they were their own chicks. Kittens can be moved into the litters of strange cats and puppies into the litters of strange dogs. Joeys, the young of marsupials, can be moved from one pouch to another with absolutely no question of being rejected.

And not only can these transfers be made within species but cats have been made to mother rats; dogs have mothered cats; rats have mothered mice. Researchers have swapped red kangaroo joeys with gray kangaroo joeys and kangaroo joeys with wallabies. No wonder researchers were slow to catch on.

But as biologists made more and more transfers, a telling trend began to emerge. The chicks of altricial birds can only be moved from nest to nest when they are very young. When they are close to fledging and have begun to give their own unique signature calls, foster parents will refuse to feed them. Similarly, kittens and puppies can only be swapped before they have begun to move about on their own. Kangaroo joeys will only be accepted by foster mothers if they are young enough to be permanent residents of the pouch. As soon as they start to venture from the pouch (at 190 days of age for the red kangaroo, for instance), the mother allows only her joey to reenter her portable nest.

And, of course, this makes beautiful sense. Parental care is exclusive, but parents only recognize their own young and reject strange young when there is a chance that a mix-up might occur and their valuable parental care might be misdirected. For sheep, on the move within hours after birth, the chance of a mix-up begins at birth and so, therefore, does recognition. For precocial birds that leave their nest soon after hatching, recognition begins at hatching, and even before, with calls that the young emit while they are still in the egg.

But for kangaroos, recognition and the chance of a mix-up only begin when the joeys start to explore the world outside the pouch and to fraternize with other joeys. For bluebirds, they only begin when the nestlings leave the nest and take to nearby trees, where the bluebird parents will continue to feed them. For cats and dogs, they only begin when the kittens and puppies start to wander away from their litters.

Natural selection is obviously lazy that way. It doesn't devise or maintain systems—recognition systems or any other kinds of systems—for situations that don't exist. This has nothing to do with intelligence, mind you. Crows are among the most intelligent of birds, yet they have been known to incubate a golf ball. And why shouldn't they? Golf balls don't appear in their nests often enough that crows have been *allowed* to see the difference between a golf ball and an egg. Like the parents of other altricial chicks (and of altricial mammals, like cats, dogs, and rodents), they start off by recognizing their nest, not its contents. That is enough, usually, to ensure that they will not attend the eggs or the nestlings of some other bird. "Be kind to any baby bird in your nest" is the rule most bird parents are guided by, at least at first. This rule leads to the total neglect of any chick so unlucky as to fall outside the nest, but, by and large, it is sufficient to prevent the misappropriation of parental care.

"Be kind to any baby bird in your nest" does, however, leave birds open to exploitation by the greatest cheaters of all, the brood parasites, birds that lay their eggs in the nests of other birds and rely on them to raise their chicks. These parasites, like the cuckoo and the honeyguide in Europe and the brown-headed cowbird in the United States, take advantage of this rule and the loophole in parental care that it creates: the lag time in recognition. Their method of reproduction is not without its costs—brood parasites tend to lay many more eggs than their solicitous, caregiving counterparts—but their strategy is a successful one as long as there are not too many other cheaters around.

Every aspect of brood parasites' reproductive biology tends to be colored by its swindling nature. Their calls are simple because their young must acquire the song of their species entirely by inheritance (they don't have their parents around to learn from). The shells of their eggs are thick because the eggs are often dropped in nests rather than laid. The birds are able to lay eggs extremely quickly, sometimes in less than ten seconds, and with nearly no labor. And some brood parasites have an unusually extrusible cloaca, which allows them to place eggs in crevices or holes too small for them to enter.

Birds are not the only animals that are vulnerable to brood parasites. Any animal that lays eggs and cares for them is a potential dupe. In North America, the nests of sunfish are parasitized by minnows and shiners; in Lake Tanganyika, the mouth-brooding cichlid fish is parasitized by a catfish. The catfish lays her eggs at the same time as the cichlid female, so when the cichlid father picks up his mate's eggs to brood in his mouth, he picks up eggs of the catfish as well. The catfish eggs hatch first, though, and the catfish fry feast on the cichlid eggs inside the cichlid father's mouth.

Caregiving insects are also vulnerable to brood parasites. The cuckoo wasp, which parasitizes the pipe-organ mud-daubing wasp, lurks outside the pipe-organ wasp's nest, waiting for an opportunity to slip in and lay an egg. The pipe-organ wasp does not care for or even see its larvae after hatching, but it does provide for them ahead of time by provisioning the nest—a tubular mud construction attached to the side of a building, cliff, or plant—with spiders and other insects that it catches, paralyzes, and drags inside. If the cuckoo wasp succeeds in getting inside this nest, it will lay an egg that will hatch before that of the pipe-organ wasp. Its larva will then eat the pipe-organ wasp's larvae before beginning on the well-stocked larder.

The ways of brood parasites are wily, but, as one might expect, from a Darwinian perspective, from John Maynard Smith's concept of evolutionarily stable strategies, brood parasites rarely have the last word. Like any behavior, the ability to recognize one's young can change if it needs to. As soon as parasites begin to have a significant adverse effect on their hosts' reproductive success, natural selection starts to favor those animals that can outwit the parasites. In England, the birds that cuckoos parasitize most often, meadow pipits, reed warblers, and pied wagtails—are all able to discriminate between their eggs and those of the cuckoo.

Then how can the cuckoo continue to parasitize these birds? you might ask. For the simple reason that the competition between parasite and host has not stopped there. As hosts became more discriminating, cuckoos became cleverer in disguising their eggs, and they now lay imitations that are good enough to fool most human observers and most birds: brown eggs in meadow pipit nests, greenish eggs in reed warbler nests, and pale grayish white eggs in the nests of pied wagtails.

For a long time, bird biologists were puzzled as to how this was possible. How one species of bird in one part of the world could lay such different-colored eggs. Now it is known that in any given area the cuckoo population consists of reproductively isolated subgroups, which have been called gentes. Females within a gente restrict their parasitism to a particular host. Any individual female, therefore, always lays the same colored eggs, which match those of the host in the nest where she herself hatched. As a chick she spent her time in the nest learning the habits of her foster parents, her later hosts: their song, the kind of nest they build, the kind of site they chose to build in.

In other parts of the world, populated by other species of brood parasites, competition between parasites and hosts has developed along different lines, sometimes leading to imitation of the young rather than the egg. The long-tailed cuckoo of India parasitizes crows, and when its hatchling is in the crow's nest, its feathers are black like those of a young crow. As soon as the young cuckoo leaves the nest, though, it sheds those black feathers in favor of the brown plumage that it will wear for the rest of its life. A parasitic weaverbird that lays its egg in the nest of a warbler hatches a chick that resembles a warbler chick. Or, at least, the top half of it does. Turn the weaverbird chick over—something its foster parents would never think of doing—and its belly looks completely different from that of the warbler. Because the chick hasn't needed to evolve matching plumage on its stomach, it hasn't done so.

Not all the competitions between brood parasites and their hosts have gone so far. Not all the victims have developed powers of discrimination. Not all the parasites are sophisticated mimics. In England, the dunnock or hedge sparrow (the bird with the bizarre variety of household arrangements) has no defenses against the cuckoo, and Nicholas Davies suggests that this may be because the dunnock is a fairly recent victim and so is lagging behind in its counteradaptations. When Davies uses the word *recent,* he is talking about an evolutionary time frame—not a human one. Cuckoos parasitized dunnocks in Shakespeare's and Chaucer's times, as is evident from Chaucer's *The Parlement of Foules* (1382), in which the merlin chastises the cuckoo, "Thow mordrer of the heysugge on the braunche that broghte thee forth! Thou rewtheless glotoun!" and from the passage in *King Lear* (1608) in which the Fool warns Lear that his daughters will prove to be his ruin if he continues to dote on them, just as "the hedge-sparrow fed the cuckoo so long, that it had its head bit off by its young."

In this country, the brown-headed cowbird parasitizes more than 350 species and subspecies of birds, but only about a third of those have evolved any kind of defense. The catbird, robin, and kingbird consistently reject parasitic eggs, but the red-winged blackbird, phoebe, and barn swallow accept them. The yellow warbler doesn't throw eggs out of its nest, but it sometimes covers them up with extra nest linings. One yellow warbler nest had six stories and eleven cowbird eggs in it. Hooded orioles have been known to build an addition onto a nest that has been parasitized. In this addition, they raise their own brood, leaving the cowbird's egg unattended and unhatched.

For its part, the cowbird has not evolved any egg color or chick mimicry, leading ornithologists to wonder why this truce, this stand-off exists. Again, it is suggested that the problem of parasitism may be fairly recent. Those birds that have evolved rejection responses tend to have large bills (all the better to throw foreign eggs overboard). This and chance dissimilarities between their eggs and those of the parasite have probably played important roles in their evolution of rejection.

Brood parasitism does not require two species, of course. Remember the bluebird females, surreptitiously dumping eggs in the nests of other bluebirds. When parasitism occurs within a species, it is especially difficult to detect, since the eggs and chicks are almost always identical. Cliff swallows of the American West are probably the greatest practitioners of intraspecific parasitism, as it is called, the art of stealing parental care from members of one's own species. Living in dense colonies under bridges, highway culverts, and rocky overhangs, cliff swallows have plenty of opportunities for this kind of behavior. A female has many close neighbors, and if she is quick, she can slip into one of their nests and lay an extra egg. She will do this when she can get away with it.

Cliff swallows also have a second trick for extracting parental care from their neighbors, a trick which the ornithologists Charles and Mary Brown discovered only after years of observing these birds. Every once in a while they saw a female flying from one nest to another with a small, white object—an egg—in her beak. When she came out of the second nest, she no longer had the egg.

The Browns' explanation for this cliffside approach to motherhood is the fact that in the swallows' natural nesting habitat, nests are often destroyed by rock slides and inclement weather. If a swallow does not put all her eggs in one basket or nest, her odds of having at least some of her young survive are better. Between egg dumping and egg transfer, they estimate, 22 to 43 percent of nests in the largest colonies contain foreign eggs.[1]

Among cliff swallows, then, there is no one way to be a parent. Females incubate some of their eggs and brood and feed some of their chicks for weeks after hatching, but they foist others upon unsuspecting neighbors. Clearly, the question for the cliff swallows is not "Where are all my children so that I can care for them all tenderly?" but rather "Are all the children for whom I am caring mine?" These questions are as different as *The Adventures of Ozzie and Harriet* and *Roseanne,* and they lead to radically different expectations of how parents behave. Animal parents have been selected to provide care to their offspring, but they have also been selected to steal care when they can—from their mates, from other males or females, from other species. When I think of the cliff swallows I think of the sister of a friend of mine, a woman whose four children all live with relatives. She takes care of none of them. Is this an anomaly of human behavior? A travesty of motherhood? Or is this the best reproductive strategy of a woman who is barely able to care for herself? Egg dumping *Homo sapiens* style.

The cliff swallows, as I've said, use begging calls to recognize their chicks while they are still in the nest. Bats use sound and smell to locate their pups in the crèche; ewes use sight, sound, and smell to identify their lambs. Animals solve the problem of recognition in different ways, using the senses they have. One wouldn't expect the mole, with eyes the size of pinpricks, to recognize its young by sight or birds, most of which lack a sense of smell, to use olfactory signals.

The senses used in recognition vary, too, with the style of infant

care. Vocalizations are particularly important in animals with precocial young, young that can move around at birth, since cries can be
heard from a distance and are less subject to interference than is either sight or smell (though they are not always as precise). The birth
of a dolphin or a whale is characterized by constant vocalizations, for
these mothers and their infants have little time to learn how to recognize each other before they face the possibility of separation. And
they must rely primarily on sound. They are unable to smell (they
have dedicated their noses to breathing), and visibility in the water is
often poor. A steady stream of bubbles rises from their nursery below
the waves as the mother emits her clear, loud signature whistle, and
the infant answers her, faint and quavery at first.

Given all that is riding on the answer to the all-important question
"Is this lamb or pup or chick mine?" it's also not surprising that more
than one sense is often involved in recognition. In most animals, offspring must jump several hurdles before they are allowed into the
sanctum sanctorum of parental care. At a distance, a ewe relies on visual and auditory cues, but before she will accept a lamb at her udder,
she must smell a specific smell.

Few recognition systems are without their costs as well as benefits.
Odors and vocalizations can alert predators as well as parents, and
some animals have dealt with this by making the scent of their young
so light that only they can detect it. Coyotes and dogs often fail to notice an elk calf, even at close quarters, but the elk mother uses this
same scent for identification, slowly smelling the calf's tracks and the
calf before accepting it as her own.

Visual cues are a problem in that offspring are always changing.
They grow; they change color; they sprout feathers; they open their
eyes. Primates, with a well-developed visual sense, rely on facial
expression rather than body shape and coloration for recognition,
and some primate mothers spend the hours after childbirth gazing
into the eyes of their infants. This behavior is important for the
long-lasting attachments that primate mothers have for their young,

and it is also one of the means by which these mothers recognize their young.

On the maternity floors of hospitals, in birthing centers, and in private homes, human females who have just given birth also take part in this ancient game of survival, *Know Your Own Child.* Many women realize that they can recognize their infants by sight shortly after birth, but few are aware of how involved the other senses are as well.

Just one day postpartum, most mothers are able to identify the hunger cries of their infants, each picking her wailing baby out of a lineup of eight. They are able to recognize these cries even in their sleep, as one study of mothers who roomed together in the hospital found. The women were asked to record how often they woke at night and in response to whose baby. During the first few nights, they reported waking in response to their own babies 58 percent of the time, but on subsequent nights they were aroused only by their own babies 96 percent of the time.

Smell, too, is important. Six hours postpartum and after just a single thirty-minute exposure to their infants, 61 percent of human mothers can identify their babies by smell alone, picking them out of a group of three similarly washed and clothed infants. Additional exposure did not improve the mothers' ability. Nor did it seem that they were picking their infants out on the basis of familiar family smells, since fathers were much less successful at this than mothers. Fathers were able to recognize their infants only 37 percent of the time, just about what one would expect on the basis of chance alone.

In experiments in which clothing was used instead of infants, the mothers fared even better. After an average of twenty-three hours' exposure, sixteen blindfolded mothers out of twenty were able to distinguish the cotton vests that had been worn by their infants, choosing them from groups of three similarly soiled cotton vests. Some researchers have interpreted these findings as evidence for Klaus and

Kennell's maternal sensitive period, and without a doubt human mothers are exquisitely sensitive to stimuli from their infants at the time of birth. But this sensitivity can serve the purpose of recognition rather than bonding or attachment. A mother may still be feeling somewhat ambivalent about her infant (the deep bond that will carry them through twenty years of child care has not yet been forged), yet the infant is imprinting itself on each of her senses. She may not be 100 percent committed to this child, but she needs to know that the child she does commit to is her own.

While parents are learning to recognize their young, most young are also learning to recognize their parents, but for very different reasons. A bat pup or human infant has no inbuilt, genetic reason to care who supplies it with milk and warmth so long as some adult does, but if parents are being picky about where they direct their care, it's usually in the infant's best interest to recognize its parents. Lambs that approach mothers other than their own are turned down with an emphatic butt; a duckling that follows the wrong duck will later be driven off and left to starve.

To recognize their parents, infants use many of the same sensory channels that their parents use, but the differences are usually revealing. Lambs rely on sound and sight but not smell. This seems curious at first, but a lamb that gets close enough to a ewe to identify it on the basis of smell risks a serious rebuke if it is wrong.

The timing of recognition can also be the same, or it can vary in interesting ways. One wouldn't expect altricial infants, born with their eyes and ears closed in the safety of a nest or burrow, to be able to recognize their parents for some time. And indeed they can't—recognize either their parents or the smells of their nest. All they need to know in their first weeks of life is how to whimper when hungry or to open their mouths wide and peep. Once altricial infants become capable of independent motion, though, once they face the risk of wandering away from their nest, recognition—of either the parents or the nest—begins. In rats, mice, and gerbils, the problem of wandering infants is solved with the use of olfactory tethers, specific odors which the young recognize and to which they are irresistibly drawn. Produced by the mothers, these odors are strongest in the nest and tend, therefore, to keep the young close to home.

❦

If recognition, what we might call parental certainty, is the key that unlocks parental care, then how does one explain the many times animals have been observed caring for young other than their own? The northern elephant seal on the beaches of California that allows strange pups to nurse. The young langur that grooms and carries another mother's infant. The lioness that permits any of the cubs in her pride to suckle and may have cubs from four different litters occupying her four teats. The African elephant that cares for the young of other females in her herd, circling them in times of danger, digging them out of mudholes, nursing them. Aren't they all strong evidence that animals do not always act in ways that coincide with their genetic interests, evidence against Darwinism and the theory of the selfish gene? Or is something else going on here? Kin selection, perhaps, or a case of mistaken identity?

Adoption and communal care of young, like insect sterility, were thorns in Darwinism's side. They were issues that had not yet been resolved in 1976, when Richard Dawkins published *The Selfish Gene,* and in that book Dawkins called adoption "a double mistake, since the adopter not only wastes her own time; she also releases a rival female from the burden of child rearing and frees her to have another child more quickly." Dawkins wisely suggested that researchers look into how often adoptions actually take place and how related the parties are before giving up on a Darwinian, selfish-gene explanation.

Since then the techniques of blood protein analysis and DNA fingerprinting have become available, and researchers have done just that. And, as Dawkins suspected, the closer they have looked at these phenomena, the less the phenomena defy the law of the gene. Where adults routinely take care of offspring other than their own—herds of elephants, prides of lions, packs of dogs, hives of bees—caregivers have many genes in common with the infants. In a wasps' nest, as we know, the caregivers (the sterile sisters) are even more related to the offspring than they are to their parents. Herds of elephants and prides of lions are also closely related by matrilineal descent. The core of a lion pride is five to nine adult females that are at least as closely related as cousins. So the lioness who nurses another lioness's cub is doing her own genes good. She is increasing her inclusive fitness, as a Darwinist would say, her share of the gene-pool pie. Likewise, in packs of hunting dogs and wolves, where the pups of a single mating pair, the alpha pair, are reared by the entire pack of animals, there is a high degree of kinship.

Even in animals where adoption and communal care are somewhat rare, the parties to these behaviors are much more related than biologists first imagined. Adoption is known to occur in macaques, chimpanzees, and baboons, but all these animals live in social groups with a high degree of matrilineal kinship. In groups where the relationships between individuals have been carefully delineated through years of observation (Jane Goodall's chimpanzees, for example), adoption, when it occurs, is most likely to take place between two very closely related individuals. The most likely individual to care for an orphaned chimpanzee is the orphan's older sister.

Then there are those species in which birds other than parents help to raise a brood. At one time it was thought that these cooperative breeders or helpers-at-the-nest, as they are called—birds like the Florida scrub jay, the acorn woodpecker, and the splendid fairy wren—were practicing a kind of avian birth control. The helpers were holding off on reproducing, it was said, so as not to overtax the resources of the species as a whole. But now that it is known that the helpers in these species are usually the earlier offspring of the parent birds, biologists have a much simpler explanation for their behavior. In species with this kind of cooperative breeding, reproductive opportunities have been found to be limited in some important way (the number of available nesting sites, for example, or a scarcity of food supplies), and young birds do better, genetically speaking, by helping their parents raise their siblings than by trying to establish nests of their own. At the same time, they are learning how to raise chicks and how to compete with others of their species for those limited resources. In Florida scrub jays, many helpers-at-the-nest are one-year-olds, and the frequency of helping declines as the age of the birds increases.[2]

But there are also cases of adoption and communal care that do not obey the law of the gene, and some of these have been attributed to parental learning curves. In certain environments, raising an infant is so difficult that parents have been found to benefit enormously from the practice that an adopted infant gives them. In colonies of emperor penguins, where fathers must master the tricky business of balancing an egg on their feet while shuffling to conserve heat, many would-be brooders stand around, impatiently waiting for the chance to take over an egg. Because emperor penguins develop the urge to brood before they become sexually mature, there are always many more brooders than egg layers in these colonies, ten to twelve for every egg. When a chick hatches, these would-be parents squabble shamelessly over the right to look after it, sometimes wounding the chick, or even trampling it to death.

A parental learning curve has also been cited as a factor in the play mothering or aunting behaviors of some primates, forms of substitute child care that fall far short of adoption and that are common in squirrel monkeys, rhesus monkeys, vervets, tamarins, langurs, and stump-tailed macaques. For primates, as we know, raising a child is a long and demanding job, requiring substantial feeding and interactive skills. Prior experience with mothering—which females can get through baby-sitting or play mothering—often has a dramatic effect on infant survival. In studies of captive cotton-top tamarins—tiny, six-inch monkeys from Colombia that live in small groups which cooperate fully in raising the twin offspring of just one breeding pair—a mother who has had no prior experience with infants is certain to wind up killing, abusing, or fatally dropping her young.

Another form of communal care that is quite common in the animal world and that has been found to be based on something other than genetic relationships is the formation of crèches or baby-sitting groups in which one or two adults guard a large number of young while the rest of the adults go off to feed. Killer whales practice this, as do bottle-nosed dolphins, mountain pronghorns, flamingos, and bison. This kind of day care is far less time-consuming than adoption, far less energetically costly than communal nursing, but still one wouldn't expect it to emerge unless it had benefits for both the baby-sitter and the parents, who, freed from the responsibility of child care, can forage more efficiently.

But as Robert Trivers argued in his very first paper on animal behavior, there is no reason why reciprocal altruism of this type—altruism not necessarily based on kin selection—cannot evolve as long as a species is long-lived, capable of recognition, and stays in fairly permanent groups, criteria met by the crèche-forming animals previously mentioned. And by humans, of course, those masters of reciprocity, in child care as in every other arena of life. We have even invented money so that we can extend the webs of obligation well beyond our immediate social groups.

Most child care in humans, like most adoption, is carried out by close relatives, but adoption and child care between unrelated individuals are also common. Many of these adoptions have practical reasons. Agricultural families can always use an extra hand to harvest crops or manage livestock; in the harsh climate of the Arctic, where hunting is difficult and unpredictable, adoption strengthens ties between Inuit families and provides a basis for food sharing. But all are facilitated by the loose attachment of human mothers and their infants at birth and by the human being's great capacity for love and long-term attachments. Much adoption in our species, I would suggest, is a spillover of this ability to form attachments. It may not always make genetic sense, but natural selection might well put up with it (as long as it doesn't happen too often) because the ability to form attachments is so important to human cooperation and success. Indeed, it is hard to imagine that we could be built otherwise, that we could possess such capacities for love and affection yet direct them, invariably, toward only our own offspring.

❧

Not all adoptions or communal care in the animal world make sense, though, genetic or otherwise. Mistakes also happen. The free-tailed bat mother tries to avoid giving milk to pups other than her own, but sometimes a pup is just too persistent and quick. The herring gull is known for its viciousness toward the chicks of other gulls, but when it carries a chick back to its nest to eat and that chick is still alive, sometimes it gets confused. It can't immediately recognize its own young, after all, and, rather than risk eating one of them, it adopts the strange chick instead.

Recognition systems can also cause mistakes for other reasons. They allow parents to identify their young under one set of environmental conditions, but when those conditions change, parents may make errors in dispensing care.

A good example of this is the Californian rookeries where large numbers of northern elephant seals come ashore to give birth. The preferred place for a female elephant seal to whelp is a sandy beach on a small offshore island. There, amid a fairly small number of other elephant seals, these enormous mothers give birth to their single black-furred pups, warbling as they are born and touching the pups' noses with their own as they warble in return. But because the population of northern elephant seals has increased steadily since this species was protected in 1892 (a time when the seals had been hunted nearly to extinction), such idyllic nurseries are in great demand. Seals now give birth on the mainland, in large, crowded rookeries where their recognition system, perfectly adequate for an isolated island, is far from precise.

Now when a mother elephant seal returns from the sea and hauls out on the beach, she calls loudly for her pup as she wades into a bedlam of roaring, heaving animals: 7,000-pound bulls who circulate in search of conquests, 2,000-pound mothers, and their 65-pound pups. Mothers try to find their pups in this confusion by listening for their particular warbling sound and smelling their particular smell, but they often make mistakes. A mother may ignore her own pup and nurse someone else's. Or she may adopt a second pup, with disastrous results. Since an elephant seal produces only enough milk for one pup, both pups usually starve.

In the California rookeries, this self-defeating behavior is rampant, but seal mothers that can somehow recognize their pups, even under these difficult conditions, will still have the genetic upper hand. It is their superior pup-recognizing genes that will survive, and their behavior that may become the norm as the seals adapt to their changed environment. And to those of us who think of the world as a static place and of evolution as a phenomenon of the past, these elephant seals are a reminder: circumstances are always changing—and our behavior along with them.

VIII

Nesters, Cachers, Carriers, and Followers

The maternity ward of the New York Aquarium (officially the Aquarium for Wildlife Conservation) is a large, round pool with observation windows cut into its sides and filled with 400,000 gallons of seawater. Like the rest of the aquarium, it lies across the street from the Cyclone, the Coney Island roller coaster. In the pool, in early June 1994, a fourteen-year-old beluga whale that the aquarium staff calls Natasha circled repeatedly, silently dipping and diving with infinitely more grace than the mechanical contraption next door. Natasha was fifteen months pregnant, one month to go. She was due to give birth at the end of June or the beginning of July, about the same time belugas in the wild gather in the warm, shallow waters of the St. Lawrence estuaries to give birth, folded fluke first, to their single precocial calves.

The calves will be gray at first, not the startling white of their mothers (a white that blends in well with the ice floes of their Arctic habitat and that has given them their name, *beluga,* from the Russian *belukha* or "white"), but they will have the same curled lips (which give the impression that they are always smiling) and the same melon-shaped heads, allowing them to produce the same incredible range of sounds. Called sea canaries by sailors, these gregarious animals have had their sounds likened to birdcalls, ringing bells, bulls' bellows, pigs' grunts, rusty hinges, horses' whinnies, and babies' cries, as well as snores, screams, whistles, and the putt-putt of motorboats. The belugas use these sounds to recognize and communicate with one another and to find breathing holes in the deep dark of the Arctic winter by echolocation, bouncing sound waves off the ice.

Natasha would not be the first beluga to give birth at the New York Aquarium, but she was one of fewer than ten, and the aquarium researchers were far from nonchalant about her progress. The fourteen-foot whale had been trained to present her fluke so blood samples could be taken (they will be used to piece together the hormonal score of a beluga pregnancy) and to come to the surface and roll over, to "lay out," in aquarium parlance, for periodic ultrasounds of the developing fetus. "We would also like to track weight gain over the course of her pregnancy," observed Kevin Walsh, director of mammal training and the man responsible for getting Natasha and the other Coney Island belugas to cooperate with their obstetricians, "but we don't want to stress her too much."

Walsh, a friendly chain-smoker who has been in the business of training animals since the age of fourteen, was dressed for work in a wet suit as he told me about the reproductive biology of the beluga whale that day in June. Most of the beluga births had been successful, he said, though one infant was stillborn and a second swam into the wall of the pool and died. One potentially fatal situation was caused by the staff themselves when they put a second beluga female into the birthing tank to help the mother. "The staff had observed dolphins acting as midwives to other dolphins and thought that belugas might do the same," Walsh explained. "But instead of helping, the female tried to attack the newborn."

Different strokes for different species, I thought. Even biologists have to remind themselves of this basic truth. Birth is difficult for dolphins, and stillbirths are common, so midwifery may have evolved in this species, as it has in humans, as a way of increasing the survival of mothers and young. Belugas, on the other hand, experience little difficulty in giving birth, so the reaction of beluga females is more likely to be that of most mammalian mothers: distance and rejection of unrelated young.

Though most of the births at the aquarium had gone well, nursing, Walsh told me, was another matter. Waiting for the beluga calves to find their mothers' nipples and to receive their first drink of whale milk, rich as a bowl of ice cream, had given the staff a collective head of gray hairs. One of the calves took fourteen hours to nurse; another, thirty-three. "We could see that the baby was trying," recalled a staff member who was on hand for that excruciating day and a half, "but it was trying on the mother's head or on her tail. It was a very difficult decision to stand back and watch."

"We have the technology to bottle-feed the babies," Walsh added. "But we don't want to."

Part of the staff's anxiety had to do with ignorance. No one knew how long this delicate operation, this throwing out of the milk lifeline, takes, in the estuaries of the St. Lawrence River. But part was also based on knowledge. The staff was all too aware of the particular difficulties that newborn belugas, like all newborn whales and dolphins, face.

Like most mammals, whales search for their mothers' teats by bumping against their bodies and rooting with their snouts. But whales and dolphins lack the advantage of smell in this search. They cannot follow a pheromone trail to the teat, as land mammals do, because long ago their ancestors traded in the ability to smell for the ability to live the aquatic life. Noses migrated to the tops of these pioneers' heads and became their blowholes.

Then there is the matter of the female beluga's anatomy. The mammary glands of whales and dolphins are not like those of land mammals. They do not release milk when the nipple is sucked for the simple reason that if marine infants were to suck, they would take in salt water as well as milk. Instead, the mammary glands of whales and dolphins are made like pumps and are operated by a compressor muscle that runs alongside the gland and is under the cetacean female's control. Infants do not suck; rather, they are force-fed. Their job is to clamp onto the mammary gland and roll their tongues out of the way. Their mothers, then, compress their muscles and eject the milk. One feeding takes place in just a matter of seconds.

A naive mother, though, one giving birth for the first time, has never used this muscle before. She, too, has to learn how to nurse. The location of her mammary glands, one on either side of the birth canal, does not help her in this important task. The mother, after all, has just given birth, and her mammary glands are in the precise area where she is the most sore.

All belugas face these obstacles, but those in the aquarium, as the staff well knows, face an additional obstacle unknown to belugas in the wild. It is, perhaps, their largest obstacle and something that causes zoo and farm mothers all over the world to fail at nursing. They are being watched. Mares have rejected foals as a result of being too closely attended too soon after birth; whole herds of pigs have come down with agalactia, as it is called, the failure to secrete milk.

Most agalactia is caused by stress, the stress that normally secretive animals must feel when they are constantly observed, and observed moreover by somewhat anxious observers. In pigs it is usually cured by sending the pigman on holiday and bringing in someone who is less highly strung. But animals may also take much longer to begin nursing than their observers think possible. Malcolm Parker, the editor of a book on comparative lactation, makes clear that it is no coincidence that zoos making the greatest efforts to observe maternal behavior after birth are the ones that hand-rear the greatest proportion of their young. Parker points out that "the length of time a mother may take to come fully into milk may be much longer than is generally realized. Humans have taken as long as five days without any apparent adverse effect on the baby and many gorillas show no signs of being in milk for twenty-four hours."

At the aquarium Walsh and the rest of the staff planned to reduce the stress on Natasha as she went into labor as much as possible. They planned to have finished their current construction projects and to strictly limit the number of observers present. They even had a secret password to alert the staff, but not the aquarium's visitors, that Natasha was in labor. "The last thing you'd want to do," said Walsh, "is to announce over the intercom that a birth was taking place in the holding tank."

Natasha's impending delivery was not the only thing on Walsh's mind as he took me around the aquarium. He also wanted me to see some of his other charges: three baby walruses that had recently been rescued from an island in the Bering Sea after their mothers were killed by Inuit hunters. The walruses had been only about a week old, and still trailing their umbilical cords, when they had been flown to New York to be bottle-fed by Walsh and several assistants. But after two months of around-the-clock feeding—one bottle, 1,750 milliliters of high-test synthetic walrus milk, every four hours—they had grown tremendously and now weighed about 170 pounds each. They lay in their cage looking like a pileup on the interstate or a tackle of football players.

"Don't get too close," Walsh cautioned as I walked toward the small hill of walrus flesh. I had heard that walruses, in their bone-crushing chumminess, their love of almost total body contact, sometimes injure their keepers in zoos and aquariums, but these animals were behind bars. What could be the reason for his warning? I stepped forward again, wanting to see the stiff hairs on the walruses' faces, to find out where one body began and the other ended.

"Don't get too close," Walsh repeated in a loud whisper, and this time I turned back.

"What's the matter?" I whispered back.

When I heard his answer, I almost laughed out loud. His concerns were so familiar, so utterly human. "I don't want you to wake them up," he said. Of course. If they woke up, they'd be hungry, and Walsh, like all nursing moms, had a lot to do before the next feeding. How well I remembered that feeling. How fast the time between feedings always seemed to go. I could remember being just as reluctant to let a visitor take a peek at one or the other of my sleeping daughters for fear that she would wake up. How important it seemed then to have just twenty more minutes of uninterrupted time.

Earlier in the day, Walsh had told me that he was raising his two small boys alone. Now, as we walked away from the walrus pen, I asked him if he thought it a coincidence that he should be bottle-feeding walruses at work and a single parent at home. "It's more me than coincidence," he admitted. "I often find myself in that kind of nurturing position. I guess I've always had broad shoulders."

Natasha gave birth on the twenty-eighth of June, and when I called Walsh to see how it had gone, he said she had been an excellent mother. As soon as the calf had taken its first breath, Natasha had turned around and drafted it to her side, sucking it toward her with the turbulent pull that her swimming produces and holding it down with her pectoral fin in order to build up its lungs. Thirty hours had passed before the newborn received its first meal, but the staff did not lose any sleep this time. They had been through this before and knew now that the lifeline between mother and calf does not materialize instantly, that delivery of this magical first meal can take time.

❦

Beluga mothers in the wild nurse their calves for some twenty months, until they are about to give birth again and their young are able to find their own salmon, shrimp, octopus, and cod. As with all mammals, feeding of the young is built into the reproductive system. It is a nonelective part of parental care and the defining feature of a mammal, the most important thing that marsupials, platypuses, spiny anteaters, and placental mammals have in common.

So as mammals we tend to take the feeding of young for granted. But not all animal parents, of course, feed their young. Not even all parents that tend their eggs or young to the point of hatching or birth. Most egg-guarding fish do not for the simple reason that fish fry are so much smaller than their parents and eat food, microcrustaceans and the like, that is also much smaller than the food eaten by adults. In reptiles size is also an issue; the crocodile mother protects her young after they have hatched and takes them down to the water, where they will find food, but she doesn't actually feed them. Few insects feed their young after hatching, but some, as we have seen, make other arrangements, provisioning their cells and nests with caterpillars and spiders that they have paralyzed with their venom and stored in a state of suspended animation so that their larvae might have a supply of fresh food when they hatch.

For animals other than mammals, then, feeding is not intrinsic to parental care. Animals add it to their reproductive strategies to give them a leg up in their lifelong quest for descendants. The most vulnerable moment in any animal's life is when it first finds itself completely on its own. When it must forage and fend for itself. Feeding postpones that moment until a young animal has grown to such a size that it is better able to cope. Young that are fed by their parents become nutritionally independent at a much greater fraction of their full adult size. And in the meantime those young are shielded against the vagaries of fluctuating or difficult-to-find food supplies.

Feeding of the young may not be a sine qua non of parental care, but once an animal takes this step, its young become totally dependent on the extra effort. "In virtually all species where young are fed by their parents," notes Tim Clutton-Brock, "they do not survive if parents are removed, though where both parents are involved the removal of one is not necessarily fatal."

And like every other aspect of parental care, feeding of one's young has costs as well as advantages. The costs may greatly exceed those of egg laying or gestation. In order to feed their nestlings, most birds work at four times their basal metabolic rate, the equivalent of a human being chopping wood all day, every day. Lactating mammalian females spend two and a half to five times more energy on a daily basis than their nonlactating counterparts. In order to meet their increased needs, they increase the number of hours they spend eating by as much as 30 percent.

Parents of all stripes do their best to cut down on these costs. Nest-building animals save energy by insulating their nests well. A thick-walled, heavily insulated structure frees a parent up from the job of incubation or brooding much sooner and allows it to get on with the business of foraging earlier than one that is poorly built. As previously noted, the parents of some precocial young form crèches or baby-sitting groups so that the young don't have to accompany their parents on long foraging trips and parents, freed from the responsibility of looking out for their young, can search for food more efficiently. Flamingos leave their chicks in crèches of thousands, tended by only a few adults. Water buffalo mothers on the sprawling plains of northern Australia rely more and more on this kind of child care as the breeding season progresses, water holes dry up, and the cows must go farther and farther in search of food.

Many animals also time their breeding season so that feeding or lactation coincides with the greatest availability of food. The bluebird synchronizes the hatching of its first clutch with spring's first crop of spiders; the free-tailed bat, with the explosion of moths in Texas in June. Not many animals store up fat, or supplies, in one season to feed their young in another, but bears and penguins, as well as some insects and even a few birds, do. In Scandinavia, where breeding seasons are extremely short, thick-billed nutcrackers nourish their nestlings with hazelnuts that they buried in the ground the previous autumn and can locate in even the deepest snow. The crested bellbird, which lives in arid parts of Australia, protects its nestlings from want by gathering caterpillars before its eggs have even hatched. It partly paralyzes the caterpillars by squeezing them in its bill, then deposits them among the eggs in case a drought should later make caterpillars hard to find.

Most animal parents that feed their young feed them with the food they themselves eat, either as is or prepared in some way. Some parents, though, use a specialized diet, foods particularly suited for the young, or special secretions, like milk.

Birds typically feed their young on the adult diet: insect-eating birds feed their nestlings insects, and flesh-eating birds feed theirs prey. The food is often fixed, though, in interesting ways. The bluebird bashes in the heads of caterpillars so that the insects' strong jaws will not injure the nestlings on the way down; bee-eaters remove the stings of bees; secretary birds, the heads of snakes. Shearwaters, albatrosses, and petrels—seabirds that may fly hundreds of miles to find fish and other marine organisms—economize on trips by predigesting their catch in their stomachs, turning it into a thick, oily soup so rich that young shearwaters need to be fed only once every other night.

In some birds, though, the adult diet is not suitable for young chicks. Grains, seeds, and fruit do not have enough protein for rapidly growing chicks, so many seed- and fruit-eating birds start their chicks out on insects and lizards. The seed-eating pigeons and doves secrete crop milk, a highly nutritious substance produced by the cells lining their crops. For the first five days after hatching, squabs are fed exclusively on this cream-colored liquid; for the next eighteen, they are given milk-softened seeds.

Insects use a variety of methods to feed their young. Ambrosia beetles eat a special fungus, which they cultivate on the walls of their burrows, and they feed their young the same substance by sealing off the larval chambers (cradles, as they are called) with plugs of fungus that the mother beetle renews until the young are mature. Some wood-boring beetles give their young wood that has been chewed and partly digested; workers in the nests of yellow jackets and hornets feed their charges with finely masticated but undigested pieces of insect prey. The bulldog ants of Australia lay special nutritious eggs for their larvae to eat.

Mammals are not nearly so inventive as birds and insects when it comes to nourishing their infants. Some canids, it is true, supplement their young's diet with regurgitated, partially digested food, but most mammals rely entirely on secretions from their mammary glands. On milk, that is, that perfectly formulated substance so easy to digest that it allows mammalian young to put their energy into the thing that counts most: growth. Mammals have come to rely almost exclusively on milk because milk solves so many reproductive problems. It is the sword that cuts through so many Gordian knots. It enables young to continue growth in an almost embryonic state, yet it relieves mothers of the need to carry around large fetuses. Young may still be nutritionally dependent on their mothers, but they are mechanically independent, at least part of the time. Milk postpones the necessity for teeth until the jaw is large enough to hold a full set. And it solves the problem of dehydration, a major concern in the lives of all land animals, especially those that spend their youth hidden away in nests.

Milk also buffers the young against changes in a mother's diet, for even under starvation conditions the composition of milk remains constant. Most naturally occurring toxins do not pass from a female's digestive system into her milk, but, unfortunately, some manmade pollutants—PCBs, for example—do. Milk allows calories and skeleton-forming minerals such as calcium and magnesium to be stored in the mother's body, as fat and bone, then transferred to the young as needed—even when those materials are not available in the mother's daily diet.

Lactation may be a universal feature of the mammalian reproductive system, but it is also the weak link in that system. Mammary glands are far less efficient than the placenta at supplying nutrients to the young, so lactation often imposes hidden long-term costs on the mother. Her liver and kidneys can become enlarged, and she may lose significant amounts of calcium and other minerals from her skeleton. This loss is particularly severe in large, fast-growing mammals, such as herbivores, whose diet is naturally low in minerals. But humans feel it as well, and the risk of osteoporosis is much greater in women who have breast-fed. So costly is lactation that some scientists have suggested the mammary gland is best viewed as a parasite on the mammalian female rather than as a simple organ.

Only a few studies have been able to tease apart the costs of lactation from those of gestation, but those that have reveal just how high a price the mammalian female pays to have her milk on tap. On the island of Rhum, Clutton-Brock has compared the survival and fecundity of female red deer that failed to produce calves with those of both females whose calves died shortly after birth and females that raised their calves successfully. His results indicate that the costs of lactation are substantially greater than those of gestation. Females that went through the lactation period were far less likely to survive and bear more young than females whose young had died. And the difference in survival and fecundity was much greater than it was when females who had lost calves were compared with females who had failed to reproduce.

In a population of yellow baboons that Stuart and Jeanne Altmann have been studying in Kenya's Amboseli National Park, the death rate for females with dependent infants is almost two times as high as it is for females without infants. When a viral epidemic strikes the baboon population, it is the mothers of young infants who are most likely to fall victim. In the dry season, all the baboons must spend as much as 80 percent of their day searching for food, but a lactating mother must work even longer hours—while she cares for her infant. The infant often interferes with its mother's efficient feeding, and much of their early interactions have to do with teaching it not to get in her way. "The time-energy budget of the female baboon is tied up in knots over this issue," as one researcher has observed. "If she does something for herself, it is often in conflict with caring for her infant."

Yellow baboons do not baby-sit for one another to ease their dilemma, but they do enlist the help of adult males who are often, but not always, the infants' fathers. Sometimes it is a male that is closely related to the female. This male gives the infant scraps of food and sometimes lets it ride on him; most important, however, he protects the female from harassment from other group members, thereby allowing her to concentrate on feeding. Only the infants of mothers able to harness the support of such males have a good shot at survival. For baboon mothers, then, learning how to initiate and maintain such relationships is as important as learning how to carry their infants or how to suckle them.

Not that suckling is the easiest behavior to pull off. Ask the beluga infant, or the lamb that can't grab hold of a teat because its mother's udder is too full and wobbly or the teat is jammed against her leg, or the newborn puppy that searches blindly for a nipple, following a trail of scents, and increasing warmth, only to find, when it gets there, that there are more littermates than there are available taps.

In order to facilitate the transfer of milk from the mammary glands, most mammals have special teats or nozzles that fit neatly inside the mouths of the young. In many animals, these teats are located along the glands on either side of the abdomen. In hoofed animals, they are near the hind legs; in primates, they are on the chest, probably an adaptation to arboreal life and the need to hold an infant while it nurses. The teats of a whale are near its fluke, on either side of the birth canal, as we know, but the teats of the manatee, another marine mammal, are near the foreflippers, in what would be the armpit if the manatee had arms. When a manatee nurses, she holds her infant to her body with her flipper, like a human mother cradling a child, a sight that must have inspired many of the reports of mermaids and sirens.

Teats are not required by mammals, though. Spiny anteaters and duck-billed platypuses feed their young with milk from mammary glands, yet they lack these handy devices. Milk just seeps into their fur from enlarged pores on their skin, and the young suck it up using their large nursing lips, well-developed oral protuberances that are present only during the nursing period.

All mammals feed their young milk, though, and all milk is a mixture of water, fats, proteins, sugars, and sprinklings of various minerals, vitamins, and hormones. The proportions of those ingredients vary greatly from species to species. Sheep milk, for example, is about 80 percent water, 9 percent fat, and 5 percent protein; the milk of the great blue whale is 50 percent water, 30 percent fat, and 12 percent protein. Infants, as might be expected, do best on the milk of their species. This much biologists have known for a very long time, but they did not even suspect how milk composition related to parenting styles until Devorah Ben Shaul, an Israeli biologist employed by the Jerusalem Biblical Zoo in the 1950s and '60s, began pondering some unusual findings.

Ben Shaul became interested in milk and its composition because she often had to hand-rear wild animals and wanted to be able to concoct solutions that would simulate an infant's normal diet. In order to do this, she needed to know what that diet was. So she set out to collect and analyze samples of milk from hundreds of wild animals— humpback whales, Arabian camels, hippopotamuses, water shrews, water buffalo, one dead spiny anteater, and almost everything in between.

"I expected, of course, that the major correlations could be made on the basis of species relationship," Ben Shaul wrote in her ground-breaking paper in the *International Zoo Yearbook* in 1962, "but [I] soon found that this was not so. I found myself confronted with irrational results such as the fact that a grizzly bear and a kangaroo had virtually the same milk composition or, as another example, the reindeer and the lion."

Some researchers might have been tempted to put these findings away in a drawer, to chalk them up to contaminated glassware or an incompetent technician, but Ben Shaul persevered. As the number of her samples grew, she began to see a pattern—a connection between the composition of an animal's milk and its nursing behaviour. Perhaps, after all, it made sense that the milk of a grizzly bear and a kangaroo should be so similar, since in both species mothers are always with their young and the young can nurse at any time. The milk of both is very dilute compared with that of many other animals. It consists of about 88.9 percent water, 3.0 percent fat, and 3.8 percent protein.

Dogs, cats, and rodents, by contrast, all have milk that is more concentrated and higher in fat. But they all leave their young in nests for hours at a time, so perhaps that also makes sense. Fat, after all, has the highest satiety value of any food. Goats, sheep, and primates, whose young follow or are carried by their mothers at all times, have, like grizzlies and kangaroos, milk that is relatively dilute and low in fat.

Suddenly, Ben Shaul was able to make sense of even her most puzzling findings, the fact, for instance, that a giraffe mother produces a high-fat, high-protein milk for the first ten days of her infant's life, then switches to a low-fat solution. During its first ten days, a giraffe infant remains in a secluded spot for twelve to fifteen hours at a time while its mother forages for food. After ten days, though, the infant is able to follow its mother and to nurse as often as it wants.

In the decades since Ben Shaul's paper was published, her data on milk composition have been augmented and refined with samples from many more animals and from animals at different points in their lactation periods, but her basic insight has stood. It has been used to explain even more bizarre nursing phenomena than those of which she was aware. Kangaroos, for example, have since been found to express very different types of milk from their two teats. One type, a low-fat variety, is for the newly born kangaroo, that embryoniclike thing that will be a permanent resident of the pouch for many months. The second type, a higher-fat brand, is for the young-at-foot, a joey that is old enough to leave the pouch but will continue to suckle for five to eight months, putting its head inside the pouch to do so. What is most astonishing is that a kangaroo mother can express these two types of milk at the same time. She can nourish both a young-at-foot and a pouch baby. The joey is always sure to drink from the correct tap because its embryonic sibling is actually attached to its teat (by its mouth) and will be for some time.

In her original paper on the rationale of milk composition, Ben Shaul also recognized that milk can reflect factors in addition to child care, factors relating to the ecology of a species, to the environment in which it lives and how it lives in that environment. The high-fat milk of whales, seals, and dolphins, she pointed out, is a result of the fact that these animals spend a good portion of their time in cold water. Since then, bats, mammals in whom flight has placed a premium on weight reduction, have been found to have milk that is high in fat and dry matter but very low in water. Primates have been found to have milk high in carbohydrates because carbohydrates are necessary for the rapid brain growth that primate young experience after birth. Animals whose brains are almost completely developed at birth—seals, for instance—have milk that is very low in carbohydrates.

Seals also provide a striking example of just how intimate the connection is between milk composition and the environment. Small ringed seals, for instance, give birth on the fast, permanent ice of the

Arctic seas, and mothers nurse their infants for two months on milk that is about 45 percent fat. By contrast, hooded seals (also known as creasted or bladdernose seals because of black sacs on top of the males' heads) give birth on the impermanent sea ice of the North Atlantic regions. Because their cradle is always in danger of being broken up by storms, currents, or warm weather, these animals have the shortest lactation period of any mammal, just four days, but their milk is the richest of that of any mammal, more than 60 percent fat. During the four days that hooded seal infants spend with their mothers, they nurse frequently, about every half hour, and put on about fifteen pounds per day.

Milk is some kind of miracle brew all right, carefully concocted to meet the physiological needs of the young in the environment in which they are raised; concocted, too, to reflect how a mother takes care of her young, whether she is a nester, cacher, carrier, or follower, as biologists have dubbed some of Ben Shaul's groups. The nutritional needs of infants and the feeding styles of mothers evolved together to produce, for each species, a finely tuned solution of proteins, vitamins, fats, minerals, and carbohydrates. An infant best grows and thrives on its particular solution, and improper growth—or consequences even more severe—results when infants are fed on the milk of almost any other species.

Not long after Ben Shaul published her findings, researchers began to wonder what, if anything, the composition of human milk could tell us about humans, about the circumstances in which humans evolved and the way human infants first suckled.

Nicholas Blurton Jones, an English ethologist, was one of the first to look at this question, and he began by simplifying Ben Shaul's categories. He divided terrestrial mothers into just two basic types: continuous feeders, mothers who carry or are followed by their young and are, therefore, in constant contact with them, and spaced feeders, mothers who cache their young or keep them in nests. These two groups, as Blurton Jones pointed out, differ in certain predictable ways. Spaced feeders, as their name implies, feed their young at widely spaced intervals, and their milk has a high protein and fat content; also, their infants suckle at a rapid rate. Continuous feeders, on the other hand, carriers like primates, marsupials, and certain bats, as well as followers like sheep and goats, feed their young more or less continuously, and their milk is low in fat and protein; their infants suckle slowly.

So where do humans fit in this scheme? With a fat content of 4.2 percent and a protein content of 0.9 percent, human milk clearly puts us in the category of continuous feeders. This fits in well with what we know of infant care in the few remaining hunter-gatherer societies, the !Kung of the Kalahari Desert or the Papua New Guineans, whose mothers carry their infants (on their hips or in a sling) and nurse them very frequently (during the day as often as every fifteen minutes, and at night at least once until they are about three years old). It also makes sense of some of the idiosyncrasies of the modern human infant's behavior, such as the fact that a crying baby is quieted by rocking movements in the range of sixty cycles per minute, just the speed of a human female as she walks slowly, looking for food, perhaps, and carrying an infant on her hip. Or the fact that today's infant is noisy, in sharp contrast to the silence of most primate babies. The wailing that we've come to expect from our infants may not always have been part of their behavior pattern. Infants who are in constant skin-to-skin contact with their mothers rarely get so hungry that they cry for food. Their mothers are able to read their early hunger signals—moving, gurgling, fretting—and help their infants to the breast long before they get to the point of crying.

Colic, too, may be the result of treating our continuously feeding infants as if they were spaced feeders. When hand-reared rhesus monkeys are fed on a two-hour schedule, they vomit and burp frequently, something that rhesus monkeys fed by their mothers never do. "Perhaps the frequent vomiting and 'posseting' of human babies is a result of our insistence on the very early development of a four-hourly schedule rather than the quarter-hour and two-hour interval suggested by comparative data on milk composition," Blurton Jones has observed.

Blurton Jones is probably right, yet it is so easy to see how this change might have come about, how women, even women who loved their infants dearly, must have leapt at the opportunity to put their babies down for a while in some safe spot—a house, a bed, the care of an older sibling—and go about their business unimpeded. It is easy to see how they might have stretched the nursing interval, not to the point where the infant's health and growth obviously suffered and milk production was curtailed but to some point where the infant continued to thrive *and* the mother had a little time to herself. Baboon mothers would certainly understand this. It is the nature of every lactating female as she juggles her needs and the needs of her infant. It is the same balancing act that has led to crèches and aunting behavior, baby-sitters and communal nursing.

Humans may have started out as continuous feeders then, but, in Western societies at least, we are now spaced feeders in everything but milk composition. The fact that milk composition hasn't kept pace with maternal behavior shouldn't surprise us, since civilization, as one biologist has pointed out, may be too recent to have had any appreciable impact on the human genetic makeup. Humans have spent about 98 percent of our existence leading the nomadic life of hunter-gatherers, so we are still very much hunter-gatherers in our genes.

No one knows exactly when the change from continuous to spaced feeding occurred, but it probably accompanied the development of fixed agricultural settlements and permanent shelters. Nor does anyone know all the effects this change has had. We know that birth spacing and population growth have been greatly affected, since frequent breast feeding seems to be the key to inhibiting ovulation during lactation and, therefore, the key to moderate population growth. (Birth spacing and population growth were also directly affected by permanent settlements since women needed no longer to be restrained in their childbearing by the fact that they had to carry their infants as they foraged until those infants were approximately four years of age.) But whether this transition from constant, close contact with one's mother to hours spent alone in a hammock or a crib has affected human development and the human psyche is also a matter of speculation. Perhaps it has meant nothing more than a little colic in infancy. Then again, perhaps it is the source of our modern angst. It's something to think about the next time you hear a baby cry.

❧

In mammals, of course, the female is responsible for providing her young with sustenance. One small step in parental care has led to another, and the mammalian female now carries the weight of lactation, the brunt of parental care. In monogamous species, males may lighten her load by guarding her and her young, by grooming the trails that she takes to forage for food, or even by providing her with food, as wolves and humans do. But despite the rigors of milk production, none help out with lactation itself. Why is this? Both male and female pigeons secrete crop milk, so why don't mammalian fathers, especially devoted mammalian fathers like the marmoset or the klipspringer, help with lactation? What's stopping them from nursing their young? Are there physiological barriers to male lactation? Are males built in such a way that it would be impossible for them to produce milk?

In the rain forest of Kuala Lompat, in Malaysia, a group of American and Canadian biologists recently found something to suggest that the answer to this question is "Probably not." What they found was a large population of lactating male fruit bats. There was no evidence that the bats were actually nursing young bat pups; the researchers concluded that the milk was probably the incidental by-product of a diet rich in naturally occurring plant-derived estrogens. But the finding, reported in *Nature* in 1994, indicates that the barriers to male lactation are not insurmountable.

That is the suggestion also of previous anecdotal reports of male lactation—in humans and other animals. As Thomas Kunz, a biologist at Boston University and one of the authors of the *Nature* report, told me, "Male lactation has sometimes been seen in animals that are extremely inbred, and it has been associated with certain diseases—or their treatments. After World War II, there were a number of reports of men lactating. These men had been held in concentration camps but were then released and fed a normal diet."

If physiology is not the problem, what is? Why don't males help out with lactation? For a while it seemed that this question was in the air. Arnold Schwarzenegger gave birth to a baby girl in the movie *Junior,* and articles in the lay press debated the feasibility of male pregnancy and, by extension, of male lactation.

The question is an interesting one. If there are no insurmountable physical barriers to male lactation, then why don't males lactate? What's stopping them from making this important contribution? To pose the question as an evolutionary biologist would: Since lactation is so costly to mammalian females, wouldn't males leave more offspring if they relieved their mates of at least part of this burden?

But since no mammalian males are known to nurse their young, the answer to this question is "Apparently not."

Martin Daly suggested a plausible reason in his 1979 paper "Why Don't Male Mammals Lactate?" in the *Journal of Theoretical Biology.* Lactation is universal in mammals, he pointed out, which means that "this form of maternal care is of great antiquity" and probably antedates the evolution of male parental care in those few species in which it has appeared. When male care did evolve, "rather than simply shouldering a share of maternal behaviour, mammalian males evolved novel, indirect contributions like feeding and guarding their mate."

By contrast, in pigeons and doves, Daly continued, shared incubation and shared feeding of the nestlings probably preceded the evolution of crop milk. In this species the foundation of parental care was equality, and as pigeons evolved crop milk, changes in the crop's function occurred, most likely in both sexes at the same time.

Today in America, when meat and vegetables can be obtained by simply driving down to the grocery store, when both mother and father in many households work outside the home and share the child-care responsibilities, the ability to lactate might well be more useful than the traditional male abilities to hunt, fight, and build shelter. Couples are searching for a new equality, but as they search, I hope they do not forget the very significant contributions that (most) human males have been making all along and the important part, in the human story, that traditional male-female roles have played.

As the human family picture came into focus and men began to provide their mates with food and shelter and protect them as they recovered from their difficult births and cared for their exceptionally needy babies, it also became advantageous for males to forage more widely than females, especially females with young. Human males started to take on the risky, unpredictable business of hunting, and human females, to concentrate on gathering plants and trapping small animals. In other words, they divided up the labor of living.

Humans are not the only animals, of course, to do this. The male buzzard is in charge of finding prey and the female, of shredding it into bite-sized morsels and distributing it among the young. In blue-birds it is the male who forages closer to home, because he plays the more active role in nest defense. But in humans this division of labor has had extraordinary consequences, and the anthropologist Jane Lancaster believes that it would be impossible to overestimate the significance of its development. "With males and females specializing in obtaining food from different levels of the food chain, humans got to eat high-protein, energy-rich foods, yet they avoided the risk of starvation that most committed carnivores run," Lancaster explains. "This meant that not only could males provide for their mates during the postpartum period, but males and females could also provide for their young long after weaning."

And this, Lancaster emphasizes, is a feature of life that is unknown in the rest of the animal world. After a chimpanzee mother has weaned her infant, the youngster will stay with her for much of the time, but it will feed itself and build its own nest every night. But even the most sophisticated child in a hunting-gathering society cannot survive by its own foraging until late in its teenage years. No other parents feed their young throughout the juvenile period. No other juveniles have so little responsibility for filling their own bellies.

The ramifications of this change are enormous. Certainly the provisioning of juveniles contributed greatly to the success of humans (and to overpopulation), since the juvenile period is, for most animals, the time of greatest risk. But adult support of the juvenile period is also thought to have contributed to human inventiveness and tool-making, since juveniles, with time on their hands, were free to fiddle with the pieces of early human life. Anyone who has ever raised an adolescent can also pin much of the difficulty of that job on this pattern of provisioning. Parents today perceive that teenagers have too much time on their hands and too little responsibility. But teenagers have always had too much time and too little responsibility. This is the nature of human adolescents, the cushion that human parents have created for their young.

We tend to think of our prolonged adolescence as a modern invention, a by-product of the machine age and its labor-saving devices. But this phenomenon is the result of the human pattern of parenting, a pattern as unique as a fingerprint and one in which fathers have played a role equal to that of any other males in the animal kingdom. Today parental roles are changing as the roles males and females play outside the home change, but each sex has been important in bringing us to this point. Males may not have suckled their young all these millennia, but that's just one way to be a human parent.

IX

The Evolution of Love

In the 1950s, in a laboratory in Madison, Wisconsin, a psychologist named Harry Harlow was raising rhesus monkeys for his experiments when he made an observation that changed the course of his own research and altered how scientists viewed the attachment between mother and child. It was a revelation, as Harlow later wrote, on "the nature of love."

It all started with the hubris of the 1950s, and the idea that bottle feeding was better for babies because it was more precise and quantifiable. Harlow wanted to decrease infant mortality among his breeding population of rhesus monkeys, so he began separating infants from their mothers soon after birth and placing them in small wire cages to be fed. "We know that we are better monkey mothers than are real monkey mothers thanks to synthetic diets, vitamins, iron extracts, penicillin, Chloromycetin, 5 percent glucose, and constant, tender, loving care," the psychologist observed.

But instead of reducing infant mortality, the separations had the opposite effect. Baby monkeys placed in bare wire-mesh cages survived with difficulty if at all. Infants in cages with cloth pads in them did a little better, and Harlow noticed that these infants developed strong attachments to the pads and would throw violent temper tantrums when they had to be removed and replaced for sanitary reasons. But none of the monkeys behaved like monkeys that had been raised by their mothers. Instead of playing and exploring as monkeys do when they begin to leave their mothers' sides, or bellies, as the case may be, these sad bottle-fed creatures clutched themselves and rocked compulsively. Their actions reminded Harlow of the autistic behavior of emotionally deprived, institutionalized children. The closest he got to producing "normal" monkeys was when he placed a small, terry-cloth-covered wire cone in the cage. The infants spent most of their early weeks clinging to this cone, and, later on, they clung less to themselves.

More than a baby, a bottle, and a box are necessary to make a monkey, Harlow realized, and he set out to discover the other ingredients. What is it about mothers, he wanted to know, that is so essential to normal development? The answer that Freudians and behaviorists had always given, as we know, was feeding. The infant associates the mother with a reduction in its primary drive, hunger, and through this association it begins to love its mother. Feeding is primary in this scheme; attachment and love, secondary.

Harlow began to test this idea by giving his infants a choice of two substitute mothers. Both were dummies constructed out of wire, but one was covered with a soft terry cloth and lacked a bottle as part of its construction. It could not feed the infant, but it did offer something soft to cling to. The other dummy had a bottle with a nipple sticking out of its chest, but it was made entirely of wire. Harlow then observed the rhesus infants to see how they related to these surrogates. What he found rattled the theoretical worlds of both B. F. Skinner and Sigmund Freud but would lend much support to the attachment theories that John Bowlby would soon present to the world.

Except for the time they spent nursing on the wire surrogates, all the infants were in nearly constant contact with the cuddly, terry-cloth mothers. Clearly they were very attached to these seemingly poor maternal substitutes, for they became exceedingly distressed if Harlow tried to separate them. How strange, though. Their attachments were not directed toward the surrogate that reduced their hunger, as psychologists would have expected, but toward something completely unrelated to food.

Harlow called the thing that the terry-cloth mothers gave the infants "contact comfort," but Bowlby soon offered researchers a more profound way of looking at Harlow's results. For thousands and thousands of years, he said, natural selection has favored those monkey infants that clung to their mothers and that suffered great anxiety and distress if they were separated, feelings that would motivate them to search for their mothers and become reunited. An infant that was attached to its parent and felt this great distress when it lost sight of that parent was more likely to survive. Attachment-seeking behavior is built into the brains of infants, as Bowlby explained, and if attachment does not take place or is permanently disrupted, serious psychological consequences result. Bowlby had seen the consequences in the halls of orphanages and the pediatric wards of psychiatric hospitals; Harlow was raising them in his Wisconsin laboratory.

When Bowlby theorized about the reason for attachments, he deemphasized food and feeding—he was, remember, looking to make a break with Freudianism and behaviorism—and emphasized protection. Protection is all that the goose parent offers to its goslings, and it is an undeniably important part of the care of many parents. So Bowlby hypothesized that attachment evolved first as a protective device, a way of ensuring that an infant stuck by its parent in times of danger. An infant that was attached to its parent and felt great distress when it lost sight of that parent was more likely to escape predators.

In fact, though, because he was reacting to Freud's overemphasis on feeding in the evolution of attachment and love, Bowlby himself put far too much emphasis on protection. Attachment behavior in animals makes much more sense if one thinks of it not just in terms of protection but in terms of all kinds of parental care. Infants need their parents for many things—food, comfort, warmth, grooming, protection, education, transportation, and so on—depending on the species and the ecological niche they occupy. Only those that manage to stay in contact with their parents will receive the care they need, the care their parents have been selected to give.

As David Gubernick has argued in a book that he and Peter Klopfer wrote on parental care in mammals, if predation of the young is responsible for the evolution of infant attachment (as Bowlby suggested), "we should expect to find filial attachment in species where predation of offspring is moderate to high and minimal or no attachment among large predatory species." Instead, Gubernick pointed out, attachment behavior is found in only some preyed-upon species— primates, sheep, and goats, for example, but not mice and rats. And it is found among some predatory species that are not often preyed upon, spotted hyenas and lions, but not others, cheetahs or cape hunting dogs.

No, the ultimate value of attachment, Gubernick concluded, is not just protection. It is to ensure that parents will be able to provide their offspring with all the necessary care.

But why would parents need this insurance? Or why would only

some parents need this insurance, since not all parents and young become attached? Anyone who has ever taken a toddler to the circus or
the zoo or for a walk down a crowded street may have already guessed
at the answer.

Attachment has to do with parents staying in touch with their offspring and offspring staying in touch with their parents. Parents have
evolved, they have been chosen by natural selection, to give care to
their young. But they can only give this care if they know where their
young are. Infants have evolved to receive care from their parents. But
in order to receive this care, they must be in a place where their parents can find them. It's a big world out there, so how do parents and
young manage this?

For nest-dwelling animals, the answer is fairly simple. The young
are in the nest. All this kind of parent must do to deliver care is remember where that nest is and return to it periodically. As long as
the young never leave the nest while they are under their parents' care,
the parents need never even learn to recognize them as individuals,
or vice versa. They certainly don't need to become attached to one
another.

But for animals that are on the go—like sheep, whose young must
follow them soon after birth, or like beluga whales, whose calves
must stay by their mothers' sides in seas that darken and swell, or like
grizzly bears, whose cubs remain with their mothers for two years
after leaving the den—sticking together is more complicated. Animals can't telephone or write; they don't have police departments or
bureaus of missing persons. Yet they can be easily separated by storms
or predators or by wandering from tree to tree, from one blade of
green grass to the next.

One way to solve this problem, I suppose, would be for parents to
keep a constant vigil, always to have their offspring within touch,
hearing, smell, and/or sight. This is, in fact, what some primate mothers do while their infants are small. But there are two problems with
this method as a long-term solution to child rearing. The first is ob-

vious: how can parents ever find time to feed if they must constantly be on the lookout for their young? The second is more subtle: how can constant surveillance lead to independent offspring, offspring that can survive, attract mates, and raise children of their own? For this is the goal of parental care, of course: not survival per se but survival in the long term—genetic survival. Parents whose offspring are forever dependent on them are not life's winners.

So animals that risk getting separated have opted for attachment systems instead. These are their ways of staying in touch. Parents still pay attention to the whereabouts of their offspring (especially when they are very young), but they also rely on their offspring to pay attention to them and to signal them if separation occurs. Attachment is maintained by a host of reciprocal signals that change over time, allowing for more and more exploration and independence. The signals vary with the animal: monkey infants cling; human infants cry, smile, gaze, and, later, follow; ducklings pipe; and lambs bleat.

Not all animals, as I've said, become attached to their young or their parents. Attachment is just natural selection's way of solving one kind of problem. Rat pups in their nest need their dam for survival just as much as lambs need their ewe, but if a lamb is separated from its mother, it runs about frantically, bleating constantly until it is reunited. The rat pups have no such reaction to the removal of their mother. If she is not returned, gradually their body temperature, heart rate, and activity level will decrease, but all of these physiological indicators can be restored to normal with sufficient heat and food. The lamb, separated from its mother, cannot be quickly comforted by a familiar female or by a bottle of milk or a bucket of grain.

And like recognition, with which attachment is often confused (for the reason that recognition always precedes attachment though attachment does not always follow recognition; we recognize many individuals but are attached to only a few), attachment to one's parents appears not necessarily at birth but only when it's needed. For lambs and goslings, that moment *is* birth or hatching; for dogs and bears, it is when parent and offspring leave the nest or den together; for other animals, it is when the infant becomes capable of independent motion. It is no coincidence that the human infant first shows signs of being attached to its mother (by crying when she leaves the room and by wanting to be held by her and no one else) at about eight months, just the time when it is learning to crawl.

Without those feelings of wanting always to know where its mother is, an infant, in the process of exploring some new corner of the world, might crawl away from its busy mother and get lost, or eaten, or hit by a car. With those feelings of clinginess, an infant might also crawl away and get lost, or eaten, or hit by a car, but the odds that it will not are much improved. Attachment systems are not perfect. Like everything else about us, they are trade-offs: in this case, absolute safety versus growing independence.

I am not suggesting that the intense love and affection a human infant comes to feel for its mother is the same feeling a lamb has for a ewe or a duckling for a duck. Attachment may have begun in all these animals as a way of keeping young by their parents' side, but in different animals attachment now has different purposes, meanings, duration, and intensity. Through the process of attachment, infants of different species learn how to fit into their social structures, how to form and maintain relationships, how to communicate, and how to parent. Animals that form attachments learn how to parent, in large part, by being parented themselves, by receiving parental care. In these animals it is not enough for parents simply to provide for their offsprings' physical needs in order to raise young that will survive and reproduce. Rather, parents and their care become the environments in which their children develop, the finishing schools of their brains. Attachment may have begun as a way to ensure that infants got the physical basics of parental care, but somewhere along the way it also became essential for normal psychological and social functioning.

In all animals that form attachments as part of parental care, the loss of an attachment figure is a devastating blow. The rhesus monkeys that Harlow raised on surrogate mothers were socially retarded as adults, and they made abominable mothers. Infants born to rhesus monkeys that had been raised on surrogates "would have died had we not intervened and fed them by hand," Harlow noted. "Five of the mothers were brutal to their babies, violently rejected them when the babies attempted maternal contact, and frequently struck their babies, kicked them, or crushed the babies against the cage floor. . . . The other two 'motherless mothers' were primarily indifferent and one of these mothers behaved as if her infant did not exist." It is interesting, though, that if these mothers were allowed to have a second infant, their behavior was much improved. "Three of these motherless mothers have delivered second babies," Harlow observed, "and in all three cases they were either normal or overprotective mothers."

Even in sheep, where the attachment is far less intense and long-lived than in primates, severing the bond between mother and infant has serious consequences. Bottle-fed lambs experience many difficulties when they join their flock. When one female lamb was returned to her flock at nine days of age, she tried to associate with the other sheep but was constantly butted away and never developed the correct social behavior that allowed her to fit in. Later, when she had a lamb of her own, she did not butt strange lambs in the normal manner (although she permitted none to nurse), and she cared less for her lamb and reacted only mildly if they became separated. Her lamb often got itself into difficult situations.

By contrast, those young that do not become attached to their parents do not suffer these extreme behavioral consequences if they are separated from them, as long, of course, as their needs for food, warmth, and protection are taken care of. Guinea pig young grow up to mate and parent normally even if their mothers are removed during their short nesting period.

Wouldn't it be safer, you might ask, if this was true for all animals? If in no animals did experience form the basis for parenting? That way offspring would always get the care they need. That way cycles of abuse and neglect would never begin.

Part of the answer to this question, of course, is that in the wild parents deficient in parental care are not likely to have offspring that survive. The socially retarded monkeys and lambs that have shaped our views of maternal behavior are manmade inventions, the Frankensteins of our laboratories and farms. They would not exist in the outside world.

A more important part to the answer, however, lies in the value of behavioral flexibility. Behavior which is shaped by experience and learning can change as circumstances change. And parental care that is more flexible can better prepare offspring for the specific environment they will encounter when they grow up. Much of this preparation has to do with the physical environment and teaching the young about the particular sources of danger they are likely to encounter, but many young must also be taught about their social environment. One of the best examples of how attachment behavior can be fine-tuned to circumstance has to do with rank and how animals that live in social groups teach their young about their place in society, about the particular social environment they inhabit.

In sheep and many primates, female offspring assume a place in society just below that of their mothers and, unless there is a social upset, most will maintain this rank throughout their lives. Males, on the other hand, retain this rank only until they reach maturity and leave their natal group. These ranks or hierarchies, pecking orders or dominance patterns, ensure that a group functions smoothly and that individuals do not waste inordinate amounts of time and energy asserting themselves and their right to feed in peace and quiet. In some animals—baboons, as we've already seen—these ranks also determine what sex infant a mother is likely to have. And they can mean the difference between reproductive success and failure.

But rank also plays a role in how mothers actually mother. In sheep rank seems to explain why some ewes vigorously reject all lambs other than their own while others are less forceful, and less success-ful, in guarding access to their teats. In yellow baboons a mother's rank will determine whether she will be protective of her young or will fos-ter their early independence.

Researchers at the Altmanns' camp in Kenya came to this conclu-sion after observing how differently various baboon mothers handled the transition, when infants were about four months old, of encour-aging them to walk more and ride less. The researchers equate this time to the terrible twos in humans. "Infants throw violent tantrums, and a mother's patience wears thin," Jeanne Altmann and Joan Luft wrote in an article in *Natural History*. "By the end of the fifth month, every mother in the study group had bitten, pushed, grabbed or hit her infant." It is critical, though, that the mother enforce the no-ride rule if she is to be able to continue to find enough food to sustain both herself and her child.

But not every baboon mother begins the push toward independence at the same time. Some begin it early, and others seem to hold their infants back, causing the Altmanns and their colleagues to wonder why these variations exist and which method is the best.

The answer, it turned out, had to do with rank. All but one of the higher-ranking mothers in the baboon troop were early rejecters of their infants. All but one of the lower-ranking mothers were protec-tive. This may seem counterintuitive, but as Luft and Altmann ex-plain, "For infants of higher-ranking mothers, the social world is relatively benevolent. Other baboons are helpers—or can be made to be helpers. . . . For the lower-ranking mothers, on the other hand, the social environment is hostile. Other baboons are potential kidnappers, food stealers, and attackers of infants. A mother at the bottom of the hierarchy needs to be protective. For her infant, the risks of early in-dependence are likely to outweigh the advantages.

"In baboon, as in human, society," they conclude, "life is rather dif-ferent for individuals at the upper and lower ends of the hierarchy—and this is as true of motherhood as of any other aspect of life."

Neither of the baboon mothers' methods is the best because each prepares different infants for the different realities they will face.[1]

Attachment systems may have begun as a way of ensuring young the basics of parental care, but they are now used to shape the behavior of young in extremely subtle and important ways. From their parents, offspring learn about their physical environments, the challenges that they must meet in their lifetimes, and their social environments, the place they will assume in society. It may seem strange that a method basically of child supervision should have led to such subtlety and expanded roles for parents, but there is a good reason for this, and it has to do with sensitivity.

As soon as successful reproduction became dependent not on nesting behavior (on tending to the needs of young within the safe confines of a nest) but on juggling the needs of two or more physically independent beings, beings that had somehow to stay in touch amid a sea of other creatures and a host of distracting environmental features, sensitivity became an important attribute for both parent and offspring. Parents that were more sensitive to their offsprings' cries of hunger or distress would raise more offspring. Offspring that were sensitive to their mothers' commands to regroup or crouch low in the grass had a brighter future. In this plein air kind of parenting, so different from the nest-bound type, natural selection would have favored those parents and offspring that could read each other's signals and signal each other clearly.

In humans this sensitivity has evolved into what we call love, the emotion that sweetens diaper changes and temper tantrums and that few human parents can imagine parenting without. We will probably never know what it is that other primate mothers feel for their young as they groom them or swing with them through the trees or what a ewe feels for her lambs as she leads them down into the fields, but certainly love, that intense emotional attachment, is a complete unknown to the nesting animal that never even recognizes its young. In Sanskrit, the most ancient Indo-European language, the language

of the Aryan herders of the steppes and one of the least abstract lan-
guages ever spoken, *love* literally means "stickiness" or "attachment,"
as well as "the yielding of milk." One word, *snihya,* contains in it all
the essentials of John Bowlby's attachment theory.

At a wedding I went to recently, the groom's brother came with
his two young sons—on leashes. The younger boy, about a year old,
was held in a kind of halter; his three-year-old brother, by a strap attached to his wrist and the wrist of his father or mother. I saw many
of the guests rub their own wrists as they walked by, and I know that
at least some of them wanted to speak out and say that this was no
way to keep a human child by a human parent's side. This is not our
kind of attachment. Our stickiness depends on loving glances and attention to a child's needs, on setting consistent limits and extending
those limits as a child begins exploring the world. Our tethers are
emotional, not physical. Not too surprisingly, the two boys did their
best to disrupt the wedding. They screamed and yanked their parents about while the rest of the young children sat or played quietly
through a long ceremony.

❦

While sensitivity has long been part of the parenting of humans and
other attachment-forming animals, it was not a subject of scientific
study until Mary Salter Ainsworth, a Canadian psychologist who
worked in John Bowlby's Tavistock Clinic in London in the 1950s,
began to explore its role in the mother-infant bond. Like Bowlby,
Ainsworth had been drawn to the field of child psychology by children and infants in institutional care, children suffering profound effects from maternal deprivation. Her direct observations showed that
a young child when first separated from its mother passes from distressed protest through despair and, finally, to detachment if the separation lasts long enough. In cases where mother and child were
reunited, it was clear that the child's tie to the mother had not disap-
peared but that it had become anxious and insecure.

In 1953 Ainsworth went with her husband to Uganda, and there she continued her research. She set up an observational study of twenty-eight unweaned babies and their mothers from villages near Kampala, the capital, and she and an interpreter visited the homes of these mother-infant pairs every two weeks for nine months. What they saw convinced Ainsworth, too, that the Freudian notion of the infant as a passive, narcissistic creature was incorrect and that Bowlby's emerging theory on attachment was much closer to the mark. She saw infants that were active in their search for contact with their mothers, especially when they were alarmed or hurt, infants that seemed to use their mothers as secure, safe bases from which they could explore the world.

Ainsworth also saw that the behaviors of these mothers and their infants were far from identical. Some of the infants cried a lot, even when their mothers were in the room; others cried little except when their mothers left or seemed about to leave. A few didn't seem to care if their mothers came or went; they appeared strangely unattached. Mothers also differed in a way that struck Ainsworth as extremely meaningful. The mothers of the unattached infants were unresponsive to their babies and often left them alone, while the mothers of infants who cried little tended to respond to them very quickly. Mothers of infants who cried a lot gave their infants attention, much more attention than the unresponsive mothers, but not always when the infants signaled, with crying and upstretched arms, that they wanted attention. The attention they gave often did not match the behavior of their infants.

Ainsworth didn't publish the results of this research for some time. In 1955 she left Uganda to live in Baltimore, and there, in 1963, she began a second study, of fifteen American mothers and their infants. Did American infants also form these different kinds of attachments to their mothers? Ainsworth wanted to know. She came to classify these attachments as either secure or insecure and, if insecure, as either anxiously resistant (those were the babies who cried a lot and behaved ambivalently toward their mothers) or anxiously avoidant (those were the unattached babies).

In Baltimore, Ainsworth and her research staff visited the households of the fifteen mother-infant pairs once every three weeks for a year, observing each pair for approximately four hours each visit. At the end of the year, they introduced the baby and mother to the "strange situation," a twenty-minute laboratory setup that Ainsworth designed to assess the nature of the infant's attachment to the mother. In it the mother and child were left by themselves in an unfamiliar environment, a laboratory playroom, for several minutes. A stranger would enter and spend three minutes with the two before the mother left; the mother would return after another three minutes. The child's reaction to the mother's return, Ainsworth found, correlated almost perfectly with what experimenters already knew about that infant's attachment. Infants judged to be secure in their attachments often cried and clung to their mothers when they returned, but they were easily reassured; they soon went back to their play on the floor. Infants classified as anxiously avoidant showed little fear or sorrow when their mothers returned, but they also avoided them altogether, by either turning or looking away. Infants classified as anxiously resistant were extremely frightened and unhappy when their mothers returned, but they resisted contact with them at the same time that they sought comfort. They cried and pushed their mothers away while they signaled to be picked up.

As with the Ugandan mothers, American mothers who were the most sensitive to their infants' needs, who responded the most promptly and appropriately, tended to have infants who were the most secure in their attachments. Unresponsive mothers tended to have anxiously avoidant babies, and inconsistent mothers, babies who were anxiously resistant. Secure attachment was linked not so much to the total amount of time the baby was held by the mother, Ainsworth explained, as to the contingency of being held upon the baby's signaling for contact and the way the mother handled the baby. She reported that one of the effects of sensitive mothering and a secure attachment was the amount of time an infant spent crying. Mothers who picked their infants up promptly when they cried had, after a year, not demanding, whiny infants on their hands—as most psychologists of the day would have expected, as respected pediatricians like Benjamin Spock warned against—but rather infants who cried less and were more easily quieted.

"Infants whose mothers have given them relatively tender and affectionate holding in the earliest months of life are content with surprisingly little physical contact by the end of the first year," Ainsworth wrote in 1972; "although they enjoy being held, when put down they are happy to move off into independent exploratory play." The mothers who have been "deliberately unresponsive, in the belief that to respond will make a baby demanding, dependent and 'spoiled' " have, on the other hand, "infants who are conspicuous for fussing and crying after the first few months of life, and who fit the stereotype of the 'spoiled child.' "[2]

"Responsiveness leads to diminished crying," Ainsworth suggested, "by creating an atmosphere in which [the infant] can signal through means less urgent than crying, by fostering the development of communication and a sense of competence."

Ainsworth, it seemed, had given psychologists a new and profound handle on some heretofore obscure but essential element of good mothering. Her initial findings on the frequency of crying have not been replicated in subsequent studies, but in the United States children judged to be securely attached as infants were later found to have a long list of attributes that are considered important for successful navigation of the adult world: longer attention spans, persistence, positive affect, empathetic compliance, and social competence, among others. Children judged insecurely attached were found to be disposed toward antisocial, even pathological behavior.

Ainsworth's early research seemed to indicate that the quality of an infant's attachment was entirely in the hands of the mother, but as time went by and researchers began to observe newborns more closely, it became clear that individual babies also differ greatly in subtle and not so subtle ways: in alertness and responsiveness, in how often they cry and how quickly they stop, in whether they flail or cuddle when they are picked up, in how long they sleep and how much they move around. It also became clear that these differences can have profound effects upon their caregivers.

As Daphne and Charles Maurer have put it in their book *The World of the Newborn,* "The more quiet, alert and responsive a baby is, the more responsive the parents are, the more likely the baby is to be quiet, alert and responsive . . . a circular reaction that begins at birth and does not necessarily end." Or take a baby who cries constantly, even when picked up. How long before the mother, especially if she has had little experience with infants, begins to withdraw . . . or worse?

Which comes first, the unresponsive parent or the unresponsive child? The responsive parent or the responsive child? Or does each chase the other's tail? Those mothers who are sensitive to their infants' signals, be they for quiet or comfort or stimulation, tend to create environments in which their infants feel secure. Those infants who send signals that their mothers can easily read are responded to quickly and appropriately. In one long-term study, newborns rated by nurses as less alert and less active in the nursery tended to be those who were judged, at one year, as unattached or anxiously avoidant. The infants the nurses found easiest to care for were the ones later found to be secure in their attachments.

Relatedness has to help in these delicate interactions not only because parents have been selected to give care to their offspring but also because a parent and child, having many genes in common, might be better able to read each other's signals and predict each other's behavior. One researcher interchanged mothers and infants to produce pairs of "strangers." When he compared them with natural pairs, he found that communication was often out of sync and tended to be less elaborate and more cautious. But parents also learn to match their interactive styles to the natural rhythms of particular infants. In a study of three-month-old nonidentical, same-sex twins, each infant, it was clear, elicited different behavior from the mother.

In her group of Baltimore mothers and infants, Ainsworth had found that 70 percent of the infants were securely attached, 20 percent were anxiously avoidant, and 10 percent were anxiously resistant, a distribution that was replicated in a number of American studies. For a time this distribution was thought to be something of a universal. Then the results from cross-cultural studies using the "strange situation" began to trickle in, and issues of attachment and sensitive mothering got a whole lot more complicated—and interesting.

Researchers were at a loss, at first, to explain why studies carried out in northern Germany found one half of the infants to be anxiously avoidant or why studies in Japan found a high proportion of infants anxiously resistant. So did studies of infants raised in the kibbutzim of Israel, where infants are cared for by multiple caregivers. Either something was wrong with the idea that the "strange situation" taps into universal patterns of mothering or a great many infants in other countries are at risk for psychopathology, as one researcher put it.

Before long researchers began to see that the "strange situation" itself was part of the reason for these differences, that the reliability of the "strange situation" as a diagnostic tool rests on assumptions that are not equally valid in all cultures. One of these is that being left behind in a strange environment is a stressful circumstance for infants that activates their attachment behavior; a second is that for infants secure in their attachments the return of their caregiver is enough to relieve that stress.

But in Japan, where it was difficult even to find mothers to participate in the attachment studies so reluctant were most to leave their infants with a stranger for just a few minutes, the three-minute separation demanded by the "strange situation" evoked more stress and distress than mothers could soothe quickly. The result was a much higher percentage of anxiously resistant babies than in American studies. In northern Germany, by contrast, where mothers encourage autonomy and independence in their children at an early age, young infants are accustomed to being left alone or with sitters. There the "strange situation" did not always elicit attachment behavior, and observers were led to believe that many German babies were unattached to their mothers. Despite the fact that infants raised in kibbutzim have multiple caregivers, they, like Japanese babies, rarely interacted with strangers, and they reacted to the "strange situation" in much the same way.

As researchers used the "strange situation" in different countries, it became clear that Ainsworth's test was biased toward American infants because it reflected American norms of child rearing. It favored cultures where children are fairly accustomed to daily separations from their caregivers and fairly used to some encounters with strangers. It also reflected American norms of infant behavior, norms that researchers had not even realized existed. An American child judged to be securely attached might well be regarded by a German mother as demanding or by a Japanese mother as antisocial. As psychologists used the "strange situation," they found that different infant characteristics are idealized in different countries. And they found that the child a mother idealizes is usually the child she gets: sociable, outgoing infants for most American mothers; independent, less emotional infants for German mothers; and reserved, dependent infants for the Japanese.

How is this possible? How could mothers' attitudes about infant behavior shape the behavior of their own children? In a multitude of small but significant ways, researchers soon discovered. Mothers in Japan begin creating reserved, dependent infants by anticipating their every need. The Japanese mother quickly learns how to satisfy her infant and how to keep it from crying; she maintains almost constant contact with it, carrying the infant on her back rather than leaving it in a crib, and sleeping with it at night. The American mother, by contrast, helps to create her sociable, independent-minded child by talking to her infant a great deal of the time and by having it spend most of its time in a crib, infant seat, or walker.

But why do these different norms of child care exist? Are they just happenstance, the result of isolated populations interpreting the biological tenets of infant care in different ways? Or do these variations, like those among baboon mothers, have adaptive value? Do they increase the chance of survival, either for the infant or for the reproducing adult that infant grows up to be?

Robert LeVine, a Harvard anthropologist and author of many books and articles on child rearing as a cultural adaptation, first began puzzling over questions like these when he was working among the Gusii of southwestern Kenya and noticed that Gusii women carry their infants until they are eighteen months or older, long after those infants can walk. The Gusii have a proverb concerning the infant who has just learned how to walk, and it helped LeVine to understand the behavior of the mothers. One translation of the proverb is "Lameness is up." When children are able to walk, in other words, they are likely to be injured. For the Gusii, the main causes of these injuries are the open fires over which they cook their food. Gusii mothers recognize the toddler period as a particularly vulnerable time, LeVine realized, and they have responded by carrying their toddlers long after the age when women in other cultures let them run free.

A second African experience that affected LeVine's thinking concerned the time of weaning. When children are weaned, they are very vulnerable to protein and calorie malnutrition, and in most parts of rural Africa, where diets are low in protein, weaning does not take place until children are well into their second year. But, LeVine noticed, children who were very small for their age were weaned long after their second birthday, and children who were large might be weaned earlier, a custom that is medically sound and seems to represent an adaptation to hazards that threaten the child's survival.

"Humans do not blindly follow a genetic or cultural code in their parental conduct," LeVine concluded in 1974, in presenting his first model of parental behavior, "but are rational actors who adjust their behavior to the risks and benefits they perceive in the environment of childcare." He reasoned that in cultures with a high infant mortality rate or where infant mortality has been high in the recent past, the emphasis tends to be on physical nurturance, on soothing and protecting during the first months of life. Communication and education come later, when the child is past the stage of greatest risk.

In societies where infant mortality is low, by contrast, talking to the baby and looking it in the eye begin immediately. During one observational study, a sample of mothers in suburban Boston spent 65 percent of their time talking to and/or looking at their babies, but they held them only about half of the time. A group of Gusii mothers, by contrast, spent less than 25 percent of their time looking at and talking to their infants, but they held them the entire time. Researchers concluded that the Gusii have a caretaking style that "produces a quieter, calmer infant," in whom signs of distress or illness will be immediately apparent. The American mothers, by contrast, "have a maternal style that does not inhibit infant distress or nondistress vocalizations."

A child's expected livelihood also plays a part in upbringing, as do the parents' occupations. Mothers in agrarian countries have been found to have a far different pattern of mothering than mothers in urban, industrial areas. The agrarian, says LeVine, is a low-intensity pattern, which seeks primarily to soothe the infant and stresses obedience and quiet. The pattern of mothers living in industrialized countries, by contrast, is a high-intensity pattern of verbal and visual attention with an emphasis on initiative and independence. This pattern is always increasing the child's expectation for maternal attention, something that the low-intensity pattern does not.

How far we've come from Klaus and Kennell's search for universal maternal behaviors that begin at birth! How simplistic their thinking seems in light of these cross-cultural studies and the many subtle and not so subtle differences in the ways that mothers mother. Sensitivity is important in every mother-infant equation, but how sensitivity can vary. For the American mother, being a sensitive parent means responding to an infant a minute or two after it begins to cry. For the Japanese mother, it means responding to an infant's needs long before it begins to cry. And the Japanese mother may not be nearly as attuned to her infant as was the traditional Inuit mother, who carried her naked infant next to her bare skin and could even sense when it was about to urinate. Diapers were not necessary for these mothers; they simply popped their infants out of their amaaqs, or hooded jackets, then popped them back in again.

What does all this mean, though, for those of us who want to give our children the best care we possibly can? As in baboons, there is probably no one superior way to raise children. Mothers do well by their children when they anticipate the kind of world they will be living in and prepare them for their roles in that world. If they want them to succeed in a society's cultural institutions, its schools and its workplaces, they probably do best to stay within that society's norms of child rearing, norms, as we now know, that are always changing as the world changes, and as parental expectations about the world change.

Human infants may be able to thrive in a great variety of caregiving systems—in day-care centers, in kibbutzim, and at home with just their mothers to watch over them—but each of these systems will affect the infants in different ways; they will all leave their mark. The sensitive care that a Japanese mother gives her child develops the child's sense of dependence on the mother and its sense of the mutual dependence of society as a whole. The time that American children spend in cribs and are allowed to cry fosters their sense of independence and their self-assertiveness.

But at the same time that we recognize the great variability in human child care, we mustn't lose sight of the fact that care can fall short of what is necessary to turn out a human being who can take part in any culture. Human infants may be flexible, but they can only be bent so far before they break and wind up later as suicides or inmates in a juvenile detention home. Infants use their caregivers to form their ideas about the world they live in and their sense of self, and if those caregivers are constantly changing, as in many day-care situations, or are abusive rather than caring, "it's like looking at yourself in a fairground funny mirror," as one child advocate points out.

Somewhere in the amoebic mass that represents all the cultural variations on parenting, all the ways that human mothers tend to the needs of their young, there must be some universals of good parenting. Researchers are still trying to define those universals, but it is a safe bet that they will include some definition of sensitive care and some stability in the infant's relationships, especially when infants are forming their first attachments and until they are ready for more independence, from the ages of eight months to three or four years.

Just how many attachments an infant can make is also a matter of ongoing dispute and research. John Bowlby, who died in 1990, believed that the first attachment an infant made would be to one person, its mother, and he was criticized for suggesting that nothing less than full-time mothering will do when, in fact, other researchers have found that the number of attachments an infant makes depends on the number of relationships it is offered. This is such an emotionally charged subject that it is almost impossible to approach it without the armor of one ideology or another, but it seems likely (biologically sensible) that an infant's attachment to its birth mother or adopted mother would be its primary attachment and the one from which all its other attachments flowed. (It is difficult, of course, to test this since it is difficult to find naturally occurring situations in which an infant has more than one adult available to it at all times so that its attachment-making process can be studied.)

This doesn't mean that all women who choose to have children should give up the idea of a career and become full-time, stay-at-home mothers. For many women that is not an economic option; for others it is a path that leads to social isolation and depression—and again, perhaps, for good biological reason. For most of *Homo sapiens'* time here on earth, women have not only been responsible for child care, food preparation, and the home but have also been important providers. In some hunter-gatherer societies women provide their families with 70 percent of their total calories. The food they forage is essential to their families' survival, and women are valued not just for their fertility but for their ability to provide. Much of their status, like that of men, derives from activities outside the home. Does it surprise us, then, that women in modern societies might be dissatisfied with staying home and caring for their children? Not only does this reduced role fail to utilize many women's talents but it also seems to render them less essential to their families' survival.

Yet, because most women in industrialized societies cannot bring their children with them to work, they experience a tremendous conflict between their roles as providers and as caregivers. Time out from careers, part-time work, volunteerism, offices in the home, and day-care centers in offices are just some of the ways the modern human female is attempting to consolidate her roles, to juggle her needs with the needs of her child. Her need to work may be strong, but if she is wise she will keep in mind the needs of her child, especially during the first years of life. She will know that in the end it will be far easier to have built and launched a ship that is sound than to be trying to fix a leaky craft while it is out on the high seas of adolescence and life.

Whether a father is as good an attachment figure as a mother is another charged question, but from an evolutionary point of view, it wouldn't make much sense if he was. A father, after all, can only satisfy some of an infant's needs, so an infant who formed its first attachment to its father would not be likely to survive. There is also much evidence that females have built-in propensities for sensitive mothering. Women show a much greater sensitivity to sound, touch, and odor than men, and they have greater fine motor coordination and finger dexterity. "When these gender differences are viewed in connection with caring for a nonverbal, fragile infant, women have a head start in reading an infant's facial expressions, smoothness of body motions, ease in handling a tiny creature with tactile gentleness, and soothing through a high, soft, rhythmic use of the voice," concluded Alice Rossi in an article on gender and parenting. But Rossi also cautioned that "these are general tendencies, many of them exaggerated through sex-differentiated socialization practices."

More recent studies have found that women undergo remarkable changes in personality during pregnancy and that their scores on personality scales measuring traits like anxiety or aggression drop significantly during and just after pregnancy. "They are much calmer, and more sensitive to the feelings of other people and to nonverbal communication," notes Kerstin Uvnas-Moberg, a professor of pharmacology at the Karolinska Institute in Stockholm. "They get higher points in something called social desirability, a willingness to please others."[3]

This is not to say that any one female is going to be a more sensitive parent than any one male; nor that men should not take part in the care of their young infants (those men who do may become more attached to their children and more likely to stay involved with their families); nor that there is not an important, perhaps critical, role for the father's less sensitive style, especially as children get older; but only that on average females are better equipped for the role of primary attachment figure, a deduction that only makes good evolutionary sense.

❧

Not everyone would agree. One of the conclusions Harry Harlow drew from his studies showing that rhesus monkeys form attachments to the surrogate mothers that give them contact comfort, not the surrogates that feed them, was that "the American male is physically endowed with all the really essential equipment to compete with the American female on equal terms in one essential activity: the rearing of infants. We now know," Harlow said confidently, "that women in the working classes are not needed in the home because of their primary mammalian capabilities; and it is possible that in the foreseeable future neonatal nursing will not be regarded as a necessity, but as a luxury—to use Veblen's term—a form of conspicuous consumption limited perhaps to the upper classes."

Harlow, though, was a psychologist, not a biologist, and somehow in his optimism he failed to understand that everything about a woman's physiology—lactation, the pitch of her voice, the gentleness of her touch—sets her up for the job of mothering. Natural selection may not have linked food and love in the brains of infants, as Freud once thought they were linked, but that's because there was no need to. Until recently food and attachment figures were never separate; parenting was never à la carte.

X

The Limits
of Devotion

It is late in March, almost a year since my yearling ewe walked away from her lamb and led me down this path of parental care, deep into the domestic habits of rhesus monkeys, beluga whales, hornbills, and free-tailed bats. The sheep are in the field by the barn, just where they were last March, but, except to bring them hay and scraps from the kitchen, I hardly give them a thought this March. We did not rent a ram last fall, so none of them is pregnant and they don't need the extra rations of grain and attention. (Or at least none should be pregnant, though it is still possible that a ram lamb slipped in and did the job before he was shipped off to the butcher.) I am glad for the rest and glad for the fact that the two ewe lambs I kept from last year's crop will not be teenage mothers. But I do miss the excitement: small black surprises in among the daffodils, and lambs, seemingly lighter than air, gamboling across the fields and playing king of the castle on bales of hay.

I also would have liked to see how last year's yearling would fare as a mother the second time around, though I would bet money she would have been very competent. She is a much larger ewe now and an experienced mother. It is a strange thing, this interaction between experience and the quality of parenting that takes place in some animals. First-time rat mothers perform their parental duties just as well as experienced rat mothers. So do many first-time bird parents, especially small birds of short-lived species. Most large, long-lived mammals and birds, though, are not automatically successful at parenting. They require experience in order to do the job well. Harlow saw an extreme example of this in his rhesus monkeys raised on surrogates, deadly mothers to their first infants but adequate ones to their second. But even animals that have had normal childhoods can seem confused by and afraid of their firstborn. The young themselves may be undersized and weak. An elephant's first calf is frequently stillborn; a lioness often eats or abandons her first litter.

"Children are like pancakes," the saying goes. "You should always throw the first one out." I'd heard that saying but never really thought about what it meant or that it might apply to animals other than humans. Why should the first one be thrown out? Not because the batter is bad. No. Because the parent, the pancake chef, has botched the cooking, and first-time mothers, especially first-time mothers lacking experience with infants or first-time mothers who have themselves received deficient care, tend to respond inappropriately to their infants' signals. For humans in Western societies, attempting to raise children in increasingly isolated situations and with very little prior experience with infants, this is a significant problem with no ready solution. Perhaps infant care classes should be as much a part of the educational curriculum as geometry and American history. Perhaps, but who would ever volunteer their babies to play the role of experience in a teenager's life? (We do it all the time, of course, when we hire teenagers as baby-sitters, but that serves our own needs first and we are able to be selective in our choice of teen caregiver.)

Not that I approach these questions from any high parenting ground. I come to them from my own experiences, painfully examined and reluctantly revealed. My second daughter, I have always realized, taught me how to mother my first. It wasn't until she came along that I was somehow able to shed some of the baggage I'd been carrying around, the detritus of a fairly chaotic childhood. I was nothing like Harlow's monkeys, mind you. Maybe nobody else noticed my deficiencies. Maybe they did, but were too tactful to say anything. But I know I was harsher toward my first daughter than toward my second. Because she was much taller than most children her age (she really does take after her father), I often responded to her as if she were acting too young. My mothering was passable, but I was not able to make adjustments for the real, flesh-and-blood child before me.

Then, when my second daughter was born, I could suddenly see what I had been doing, shoving my beautiful round peg of a daughter into my square parenting hole. I don't know how Harlow's monkeys felt when they were given a second chance, but I, for one, will always be grateful. She is almost grown now, my elder daughter. She will be going away to school next year, and I dreamt the other night that she had left on a trip around the world but that I had forgotten to pack her bag. In the dream it was clothes and toothpaste and shoes that I had sent her off without, but when I woke up I knew it was the less tangible things that concerned me: common sense, the ability to resist peer pressure, respect for herself and for others, focus, the courage to meet life's challenges, and the courage to love, to become

attached to another human being. All the things that all mothers, and
fathers, worry about. All the things that cannot possibly be packed at
the last minute. Are they in the suitcase or not? How do we ever
know? When do we know? Now that I was so completely attached
to this child, I was having a hard time letting her go.

On this day in March, though, both my daughters are off with my
husband on a combination rafting and drawing trip in Texas, leaving me behind to write and think. There is a male bluebird on the
telephone wire outside my office window, the first bluebird I've seen
this year, and he looks much fuller and healthier than the ragged parents I saw at the bluebird box last July, a week or two before their second batch of nestlings fledged. I wish him luck with whatever box
he claims this nesting season (may it be surrounded by bittersweet and
honeysuckle for those hot days in July!) and whatever female he con-
vinces to join him in his mad plunge toward reproductive success.
And then I get back to the sad sight on my desk.

It is not the sight of my habitually messy desk that I return to with
sadness, but a photograph on it, a photograph that appeared in a
medical journal in an article on breast feeding in Pakistan. The photograph was taken in a clinic in Islamabad in 1990; in it a pretty young
Pakistani woman holds five-month-old twins on her lap. The twins
look so different, though, that they could be from different species,
or planets. One twin is healthy and robust, and, according to the photograph's caption, it has always been breast-fed. The other has a thin,
pinched face, sticks for arms and legs, and a great distended belly. It
is malnourished and has suffered from frequent bouts of diarrhea. It
has been bottle-fed from birth, and in the picture a bottle rests in its
mouth. The bottle-fed twin died shortly after the picture was taken;
the breast-fed twin continued to thrive.

How is this possible, the American mother wants to know? How
could this young woman have allowed this to happen?

Like most women around the world, Pakistani women say that
breast milk is the best food for babies; yet an increasing number of

them feed their infants with bottles and formula. And because formula is expensive, they cut it with cornstarch or some other nonnutritive filler. And because water is often contaminated, the babies get gastrointestinal infections and severe diarrhea.

"Bottle feeding is a virtual death sentence in many parts of Pakistan," wrote Dorothy Mull, the author of the paper in which the photograph appeared. She came to that stark conclusion after studying the infant feeding practices of 150 households in rural Pakistan. Sixteen of the mothers in her study sample switched from the breast to infant formulas with the result that five of their infants died, three had third-degree malnutrition, four had second-degree malnutrition, and four others were classified as having primary malnutrition and diarrhea.

In other parts of the world, a switch from the breast to the bottle may not be deadly, but it can be associated with significant amounts of illness and a much reduced rate of infant growth. In a 1988 study of infant feeding among the Maya Indians of Mexico's Yucatán Peninsula, an area where younger women have taken enthusiastically to bottle feeding as a supplement to and eventual replacement for breast feeding, all the infants who were bottle-fed experienced bouts of diarrhea that lasted three or more days and required rehydration therapy by a physician. None of the breast-fed babies had such episodes.

"The poor sanitary conditions, combined with a tropical climate and a general ignorance of basic principles of hygiene, provide a very unhealthy setting for bottle-feeding," noted Gail Howrigan, author of the report. "On the other hand, local physicians can and do provide oral rehydration therapy and antibiotics to treat the gastrointestinal disease that results from such feeding," which "seems to have blinded parents to the new risks their feeding choices entail."

What can be going on here? If human child-care practices are adaptive in terms of health and survival, as LeVine and others have suggested, how can we possibly explain these behaviors? Only in certain Western countries is breast feeding on the rise (in Sweden it is considered unethical to feed an infant anything other than breast milk); in the rest of the world, it is the use of bottles and formula that is increasing. And while mothers abandon breast feeding, scientists continue to analyze mothers' milk and to discover in it ever more complex ingredients—hormones, growth factors, and natural opioids—that affect a baby's growth and development, especially the growth and development of the brain.

As explanations for this seemingly inexplicable trend, both Mull and Howrigan mention urbanization and economies that take women out of the home and make breast feeding difficult, as well as the promotion of infant formulas in the media and in health clinics. In both Pakistan and the Yucatán, formula is often given out to women as they leave the hospital with their babies, and it is recommended to mothers who bring their infants to health clinics because they are ill or underweight. Both authors also mention factors specific to the culture. In the Yucatán, fathers who work at wage jobs take great pride in being able to provide their children with what they consider a prestigious, modern food. In Pakistan, where children (and especially sons) are essential for a woman's security and where a woman knows she may be blamed for a child's sickliness, shifting to bottle milk enables women to divest themselves of direct responsibility for their children's health. Along these lines, Dorothy Mull notes that most of the bottle-fed infants in her study were males.

But compelling as they may be, none of these explanations accounts for the fact that women have been giving up breast feeding for a very long time, long before the invention of formula, bottles, and advertising, and long before urbanization. No one knows exactly how old the practice of wet nursing is, but certainly it was very common in ancient Greece and Rome. (Caligula's bloodthirstiness is said to have stemmed from the fact that his wet nurse moistened her nipples with blood to make him take better hold, and Nero was nursed by a drunk who is said to have passed on debauched habits along with her milk.) In parts of the world, Africa, for example, it is still common today.

And wet nursing exists despite the fact that, oftentimes, it is or has been associated with a very high rate of infant mortality. In Africa wet nursing is one of the ways that the HIV infection is being spread. In France, where sending one's infant to a wet nurse to be fed for the first year was so prevalent a practice at the end of the eighteenth century that a Bureau of Wet Nurses of the City of Paris was established, about one half of the babies born in Paris at the time went to commercial wet nurses, mostly farm women from the province of Normandy. Yet, more than one quarter of those infants, known as *nourrissons* or *Petits Paris,* died. And that high percentage does not even include the natural children of those wet nurses, *les frères de lait,* as they were called, who must also have suffered as a result of this practice. There was a seasonal trend to these deaths, a number of studies have found. Most infants in the care of wet nurses died during the summer and the fall, during the time, in other words, when their caregivers were busy with the harvest and other agricultural chores.

Yes, of course, wet nursing was common, you might say. How else did one feed babies whose mothers had died or were unable to nurse? How else did mothers who worked outside the home in the days before pasteurization and refrigeration made bottle feeding safe feed their babies and keep their jobs? Evidence indicates, though, that there is more to wet nursing than biological and/or logistical necessity. In France in the eighteenth and nineteenth centuries, affluent women, who were not employed, also sent their infants to wet nurses, and certainly the mothers of Rome's future emperors had the time to breast-feed. Wet nursing is also said to have been the only alternative for women who were unable to breast-feed their infants because they could not produce enough milk. Many women experience discomfort when they begin to breast-feed, but actual inability to produce sufficient milk is an extremely rare condition.

And what about the very ancient, erroneous, but still prevalent idea that breast milk can be spoiled and made unhealthy, even poisonous, for an infant to drink? How is this idea—found today in China, Haiti, Africa, and Pakistan—adaptive? The oldest reason for spoiled breast milk, and one that was subscribed to by Galen and Hippocrates as well as ancient Chinese physicians, was if the mother became pregnant while she was nursing. A mother's surplus blood, it was thought, can be used either to nourish a fetus or to form breast milk but not both. As Hippocrates is said to have written in about 400 B.C., "If milk flows freely from the breasts of a pregnant woman . . . it is an indication that the fetus will be weak."

Today in Pakistan and the Yucatán, women still use pregnancy as a reason to stop breast feeding, but pregnancy is just one way they believe breast milk can be spoiled. Milk is also thought to be ruined by a mother's illness, or by her exposure to heat or cold, or to certain foods, or by an emotional upset, or by negative spiritual influences, the evil eye or black magic. Just about any experience, in other words, can be reason enough for a Pakistani woman to stop breast feeding, to stop supplying her infant with the substance most important to its health and survival. Yet scientists have found that the quality of breast milk changes very little, even under starvation conditions. There is also no evidence that breast milk is adversely affected by a new pregnancy (though it does change in texture and color, becoming thicker and yellower—like colostrum). And there is abundant evidence that it is not affected by most illnesses, or by exposure to heat and cold, or, with few exceptions, to broad beans and chocolate, by what a woman eats.

How does a Pakistani woman know if her breast milk is unfit? By testing it, of course. The same way that women have determined the quality of their milk since at least the second century A.D., when the Roman Soranus of Ephesus described a fingernail test that was afterwards used in Europe for hundreds of years. In it a drop of milk is placed on a fingernail; its quality is judged by whether it remains as a drop or flows quickly over the nail.

The fingernail test is still employed in many parts of the world, but ant or insect tests are also popular, as are supposedly scientific tests performed in pathology labs. In Pakistan in the 1990s, a woman who is concerned about the quality of her breast milk can go to an elder or holy man, who will test the milk for poison by floating an insect in it. (If the insect drowns, the mother is advised not to nurse for several weeks and then to come back for retesting.) Or she can go to a laboratory where her milk will be examined for the presence of things the technicians call pus cells (probably fat droplets or white blood cells, both of which are completely normal in breast milk) and bacteria. The bacteria can only have been swept into the milk from the skin or the collecting tube since milk is completely sterile. In Pakistan it is also said that a skilled doctor can tell if milk is bad by holding a stethoscope to a woman's chest and "looking at what was inside."

Whatever method a woman uses, though, and whatever her test results, the outcome is usually the same: she stops breast feeding. For some women a negative result does not allay their fears about their milk. For others the testing process takes so long that by the time their milk has been given the okay, nursing is a moot point; they no longer have any milk to give. The question is, then, Why are these women, and women around the world, vulnerable to concerns about the quality of their breast milk when there is absolutely no scientific basis for their worries?

No matter how many studies researchers conduct, how many questionnaires they ask women in different countries to fill out, this phenomenon—like the use of bottles and formula in unsanitary environments, like the hiring of a wet nurse whose attention is focused on the harvest—will continue to baffle us until we accept the simple but profound basis upon which parental care rests, the genetic rock that is its foundation. Parents are not genetically identical to their young, so their interests are also not identical. What's good for the child may not be in the parent's best interests. What's best for the parent may not be good for the child.

We need to be able to accept this if we are ever to understand why some parents don't provide their young with the optimum care. Why it is that they may abandon them instead, or abort them, or withhold breast feeding, either in circumstances where the infant may well die, as in Pakistan today or France in the eighteenth century, or in circumstances where it may simply do less well, as in the Yucatán. We tend to look at these phenomena as parental mistakes, lapses in care-giving systems that are generally foolproof. Few of us want to face the fact that they, too, may be part of an animal's reproductive strategy.

Though the genetics of reproduction have been known for some time—the fact, for example, that in mammals and birds parents share only one half of their genes with their offspring—the full implications of this were not recognized until Robert Trivers pointed them out in a characteristically brilliant paper published in 1974 and titled, simply, "Parent-Offspring Conflict."

Because parents and their young do not see eye to eye genetically, Trivers realized, they must not see eye to eye as far as parental care is concerned. They must have a fundamental conflict of interest rooted in their genetic dissimilarity. One way that this conflict must manifest itself is that offspring must be selected to demand more care than their parents are selected to give. Parental care is costly, as we know, and it reduces, as many studies have shown, a parent's chance of survival and the number of its future offspring. On the one hand, if a parent works very hard to care for its young, it will certainly increase the likelihood that those young will survive, but it may decrease the number of young that the parent will have in the future. On the other hand, if the parent works a little less hard, it can give its young a reasonable chance of survival *and* leave itself in good enough shape to go on reproducing.

Trivers's great insight was to recognize that parental care in any one species must be a trade-off between the competing demands of parent and young. Parents don't do everything they possibly can to ensure that their young survive. Rather, they care for them at some intermediate, compromise level, a level that has been arrived at by natural selection. And it is that compromise level that we take as the norm for each species.

This sounds very theoretical, but Trivers's thesis immediately made sense of a number of phenomena that biologists had observed, and puzzled over, in the field. The behavior of Adélie penguins, for example, on windswept islands in the Antarctic. These birds desert their chicks and return to the sea ten days before the chicks have developed to the point where they can leave their nests. During those ten days, many chicks starve to death and others become so emaciated that their chance of survival is extremely poor. Surely Adélie parents could improve their chicks' odds if they tended them for ten more days, and it seemed strange that they did not. But every time an Adélie parent leaves its nest and jumps into the sea to begin looking for food and every time it returns, it risks being eaten by one of the many leopard seals that congregate around the colony and are the major cause of mortality among the adults. The parents' departure time, biologists now realize, is far from the optimum time for chicks. It is a carefully negotiated settlement between two probabilities: that of the chicks' survival and that of their parents'.

Or take weaning conflicts in mammals and feeding conflicts in other animals, those noisy, quarrelsome, often fierce debates between parent dogs, rats, cats, lions, birds, and primates and their young about how long the parent will continue to feed the child. Baboon watchers use these conflicts to locate the normally quiet baboon troops, and many readers will have seen the threatening faces and swats that a mother cat gives to her weaning-age kittens. I will never forget one ornithologist's description of a great white pelican chick seizing its parent by the bill and dragging it to the ground so that the chick could reach in and get the contents the parent was reluctant to give. When the chick was small, the parent had worked hard to feed it, but as it matured and was increasingly able to feed itself, the parent's reluctance had grown.

Before Trivers these conflicts had been viewed as a mere consequence, or by-product, of the rupturing of the parent-offspring bond, designed to promote the independence of the young and to free the parent up for more childbearing: a step that benefited both generations. No one had ever looked at these conflicts, as one biologist puts it, "as the outcome of natural selection operating in opposite directions on the two generations." Trivers argued, though, that "the marked inefficiency of the weaning conflict seems the clearest argument in favor of the view that such conflict results from an underlying conflict." The weaning tantrums of baboons may last for weeks or months, involving "daily competitive interactions and loud cries from the infant in a species otherwise strongly selected for silence."

The time a youngster is weaned, in other words, is not the time the youngster is ready to be weaned but rather a compromise time hammered out between parent and child. For any one species, the approximate weaning time would be set by natural selection. But for any one parent-offspring pair, Trivers realized, the exact time of weaning would be affected by the age and health of the parent or by the availability of food or by signs that the offspring was ready for independence: its size or behavior or the pitch of its cries.

For these are the cues the parent uses in deciding how much care to give its young. They are also the cues the young can manipulate in order to trick the parent into giving more care than it wants to. These cues are an offspring's only trump card in a conflict with beings that are much bigger and stronger than it is. As Trivers also noted in the paper that revolutionized the study of parental care, as soon as a system of parental attentiveness to signals from its offspring evolves, "the offspring can begin to employ it out of context. The offspring can cry not only when it is famished but also when it merely wants more food than the parent has been selected to give. Likewise, it can begin to withhold its smile until it has gotten its way. Selection will then of course favor the parental ability to discriminate between the two uses of the signals, but still subtler mimicry and deception are always possible. Parental experience with preceding offspring is expected to improve the parent's ability to make the appropriate discrimination."

The effects of the genetic discord between parent and young are felt not just at the end of parental care but rather, as Trivers made clear, throughout the period that young depend upon their parents. "Consider a newborn (male) caribou calf nursing from his mother," Trivers suggested. "The benefit of him nursing (measured in terms of his chance of surviving) is large, the cost to his mother (measured in terms of her ability to produce additional offspring) presumably small. As time goes on and the calf becomes increasingly capable of feeding on his own, the benefit to him of nursing decreases while the cost to his mother may increase (as a function, for example, of the calf's size). If cost and benefit are measured in the same units, then at some point the cost to the mother will exceed the benefit to her young and the net reproductive success of the mother decreases if she continues to nurse. . . . The calf is not expected, so to speak, to view this situation as does his mother, for the calf is completely related to himself but only partially related to his future siblings."

Trivers suggested that at each and every phase of parental care, parents should be selected to make sure that the costs of care are as low as they can be in relation to the benefits. With this seemingly simple proposition, he explained another old puzzle: the three somewhat distinct phases of parental care that had been observed in species as diverse as cats, penguins, and sheep. A mother ewe will let twins suckle on demand during the first three weeks, but thereafter one twin must find the other before they are allowed to get to the udder. When the lambs are several months old, the ewe begins to turn down their overtures to nurse with increasingly emphatic butts and grunts. Trivers gave this trajectory of parental care—different in form and length in different species—genetic underpinnings that made immediate sense. Of course. The mother's behavior changes as her reproductive costs change, as her cost-benefit ratio shifts.

The cost-benefit ratio that underlies the shape and duration of parental care is not an absolute for any one species or even any one animal; it shifts as parents age and their reproductive value—their costs—decreases. One of the predictions of Trivers's model is that older parents should be more indulgent, a prediction that is certainly borne out in *Homo sapiens*. The cost-benefit ratio also shifts with changes in health and circumstances. To a parent in poor health, or a parent caught in a drought, the costs of parental care soar; the benefits, the probability of producing offspring that will survive and reproduce, fall. These parents should be most likely to abandon their offspring, and field study after field study show that is indeed the case. Brood desertion is common when animals are disturbed by predators or when food is scarce, a fact of life known since biblical times. "Yea, the hind also calved in the field," it says in Jeremiah 14:5, "and forsook it, because there was no grass."

Some of the best evidence that brood desertion can be adaptive comes from experimental studies on the effects of reducing clutch size in blue-winged teals, birds that normally lay about ten eggs. As researchers removed eggs from a teal's clutch, they increased the probability that the teal would desert (as compared with teals with clutches that were disturbed but had no eggs removed). Nests reduced to four eggs were much more likely to be deserted than nests reduced to seven. In field studies of other birds, parents have been shown to be more likely to desert eggs than chicks (to desert, in other words, at the point when their investment is less); and long-lived species like wood storks and flamingos, which will have many more opportunities to breed, are more likely to desert than birds with a shorter life expectancy.

Biologists also used to wonder about the behavior of the brown bear mother: if she lost one of her cubs, she often abandoned the second. Some thought that this was a bizarre reaction to the death of a cub, grief in extremis. Now it is known, though, that the brown bear mother's behavior allows her to reproduce a litter of two immediately after the loss instead of waiting until the end of the two-year lactation period. It allows her to increase her benefits of reproduction without significantly increasing her costs. The bottom line for any animal that reproduces over a period of years or seasons is not whether it can successfully raise any one offspring, but how many offspring it can raise over the course of its reproductive life.

So there are limits to most parents' devotion. This is one of the points of Trivers's paper, and it only makes sense. It puts the horse before the cart. In the world that most animals inhabit—the world of rain forests and mountains, deserts and oceans—children do not survive without their parents. It does no good for parents to give their last ounce of strength for their children because children without their parents are doomed. In those species which have evolved parental care, children exist within the context of that care. In the Western world, where affluence pads our existence and protects us from the knowing knife of natural selection, it's easy to forget this, to admire the courage of a bear killed protecting her cubs, to cringe at the heartlessness of a bird that abandons a nest full of chicks.

This is not to say that all parental behavior once thought to be abnormal is in fact adaptive. Pathology also exists because variation exists. There will always be individuals, brown bears or rhesus monkeys, that are deficient in the realm of parental care for reasons that have nothing to do with long-term reproductive strategies. But in the wild, of course, these individuals wouldn't be likely to leave many offspring.

❦

What does this have to do with the young Pakistani mother and her twins, with the testing of breast milk, or the Bureau of Wet Nurses? Parental care is costly and lactation particularly so, in terms of both time and energy. It shouldn't surprise us, then, that women have avoided it when they could by hiring wet nurses and, later, by using bottles and formula.[1]

Parents cut back on care when they must in order to preserve their own health, and they cut back on care when they can get away with it. Think of the bluebird female slipping into another bluebird's box and leaving her egg as a calling card. Or the cuckoo whose entire existence is built around the shirking of parental duties.

Bottle feeding, for most women, represents a scaling back of parental care, but with very different consequences in different environments. In the United States children may suffer little from being bottle-fed. Researchers have found some cognitive differences in bottle-fed and breast-fed infants and suggestions of a link between bottle feeding and anorexia or overeating in adolescence, but the effects are subtle and anything but immediate. In the Yucatán bottle-fed babies may be sickly, but most live; their mothers keep their figures and the freedom that bottle feeding gives them. Their reasons for turning to bottles are cosmetic, emotional, and practical. They want time away from the baby to work, tend house, socialize, weed the garden, and they want to be able to wear Western clothes, which are not so well adapted to breast feeding as the loose-fitting Indian dress. There will be readers who will want to tell me that this is a problem of education, that Maya women do not understand the consequences of bottle feeding. But, as Gail Howrigan has pointed out, older women in the community comment often on the connection between bottle use and an infant's frequent trips to the clinic, a connection which the younger women refuse to acknowledge.

In the Yucatán the infant pays a price in health for its mother's freedom from lactation; in Pakistan it may pay with its life. There when mothers cut back on maternal care by switching to the bottle, they generally wind up withdrawing care altogether, since the infant usually dies. And, as I have mentioned, this is usually done on the advice of an elder or a physician or a laboratory technician, for most mothers have their breast milk tested before they begin bottle feeding.

Perhaps breast-milk testing "allows the mother to stop nursing without feeling guilty or eliciting disapproval from others," Dorothy Mull noted in her paper. In Pakistan, in other words, testing and concern over breast milk may be just a prelude to the cessation of breast feeding, a ritual that these human mothers go through before they alter their level of maternal investment. And why would they alter it? Mull didn't give a reason, but in her paper she mentioned that most of the women in her study were suffering from anemia, fatigue, and malnutrition. Most were in no physical shape, in other words, to take on the significant burden of lactation.

I used to think that mothers would give everything for their children, bleeding themselves dry. I used to think that maternal behavior is an engine that runs only at top speed, an engine that is turned on by the birth of an infant. Trivers's way, however, not only makes more sense but is, in the end, kinder. Children do not exist in a vacuum but rather in the context of parents able to provide for their physical, emotional, and psychological needs. This care is not an extra, a lagniappe tacked on after birth. Rather it is every bit as important to the development and survival of the young as the months of gestation or weeks of incubation. In humans, as we have seen, this care was important in determining the length of gestation. In most human societies, eighteen years or so of care has been as much a part of the human reproductive strategy as nine months in utero.

This is not an apology for infanticide, abandonment, abortion, any of the things that parents do to curtail their investments, but it is an acknowledgment that those things exist. It is an acknowledgment that parental care is most likely to emerge when the circumstances, physical and emotional, are right, an acknowledgment of just how important, and deeply personal, the decision to care for a child really is.

Lest we in the West feel in any way superior to these Yucatán or Pakistani mothers, let us not forget how recently infanticide was part of Western societies. Overt infanticide was common in Europe throughout the Middle Ages and was not seriously prosecuted in England until the sixteenth and seventeenth centuries. And let us not forget that abandonment is still with us, that every month, on average, 1,000 babies are left by their parents in U.S. hospitals. Or that here in the United States parents ration care in yet another way.

Many children are given all the nourishment that they could possibly want, and their health is attended to in meticulous detail, but they are denied time with their parents, time necessary, among other things, to form attachments, the basis, as we have seen, for their emotional well-being, for the quality of their future relationships and the way they will parent their own offspring. Our excuse is not health but the time constraints that all parents operate under (think of the baboon mother juggling the time she needs to forage with the time she needs to nurse her infant). These constraints are made a thousand times more complex (we believe) by the demands of our culture and our social and economic expectations—great expectations! But in just 2,000 years or so, human mothers have gone from spending twenty-four hours a day in contact with their infants to two to three hours of what we call quality time.

We think that we're getting away with this because our children live through it. And maybe we are. Then again, it may be that we're just passing the costs of child care on to society as a whole, in the form of deeply troubled children who grow up into disaffected young adults. How long society can bear these costs is anyone's guess.

In today's tugs-of-war over family values and abortion rights, it seems to me that conservatives and liberals have hold of different halves of the same truth. Conservatives recognize the great importance of parental care; they see how human children benefit from the love and support of two parents. Yet they would deny a woman who lacked a partner and/or the resources to provide for a child the choice of becoming a parent. They do not see that birth, emergence from the womb, is just one point in a long trajectory of care that begins with conception and ends with a child's independence. Liberals recognize the importance of choice in childbearing, but in their emphasis on individual fulfillment and rights, they tend to devalue the importance of parental care. They tend to forget that raising children well is the most important thing that parents will ever do and to expect society to take over a larger and larger part of this job. Society can provide the economic and social structure in which human parents can express their parental care, but in no way can it substitute for the love and attention of parents. If Trivers were to rewrite this paragraph, he might say that conservatives favor the offspring in the inevitable parent-offspring conflicts; liberals, the parents.

Similarly, in the debate over welfare reform and benefit caps for women who have additional children while on welfare, liberals and conservatives also have hold of different halves of the truth. Liberals are concerned about the effects of cutting benefits to those who live in areas where there are few jobs and little economic opportunity, but they fail to see that all animal parents factor resources (food, welfare checks, and so on) into their reproductive decisions, that, of course, welfare benefits will have an effect on a woman's decision to have another child. Conservatives appreciate this effect, but they fail to see how important social and economic structures are in determining how parents parent, that all animals need healthy environments, in which they can find food and whatever else they need to survive, in order to express their parental care.

❧

I must have read Trivers's paper on parent-offspring conflict five or six times before it struck me that here, too, was my undersized yearling ewe in a nutshell. Trivers had spelled out the behavior of this reluctant mother from the genes out. Shivers went up and down my arms as I pictured her again heading off toward the hay on that day in April, leaving her lamb lying in the dirt. I had thought that she was oblivious to what was happening, that she lacked some necessary component of maternal behavior. It was unnerving to realize that at some level she had been weighing her options carefully, calculating her costs and benefits, deciding in the end to cut her losses before she embarked on the most demanding leg of her reproductive effort—lactation.

No one knows the mechanisms by which most animals arrive at these decisions, the physiological calculators that they use, though one can imagine any number of possibilities. (Researchers have found, for instance, that the male emperor penguin will continue to incubate his mate's egg until he has burned 80 percent of his fat reserves, until the moment when he begins to burn the muscle that he needs for his own survival.) One thing is clear, though: Only those animals that make the right calculations survive and leave progeny behind.

Now that I was looking at my ewe in this new way, I realized just how unambiguous her balance sheet would have been. She was young. She had a long life and many lambs ahead of her, so her costs were high. And she was small, and that would have driven them up even higher. Quite possibly she was also underfed during that difficult, stormy winter, when hay and feed were hard to find and the temperatures were unusually low. Because she was small, she might have been unable to fight for her share of food. I overruled her decision to cut her losses when I penned her and forced her to allow the lamb to nurse, forced her into a maternal behavior that she was perfectly capable of physiologically but that her calculations had told her would not pay off. Those calculations may well have been right, but in the artificial world that is my very small farm, I will never know.

Notes

II. PARENTING ACROSS THE BIOLOGICAL SPECTRUM

1. Grazers that are also marsupials—kangaroos and wallabies—are an exception, but they bear altricial young so small (superaltricial young) that their mothers can run with them in their pouches.

III. FATHER WOLF, MOTHER BEAR—WHO CARES?

1. Stamps presented this theory in a talk she gave at a conference called "Evolutionary Biology and Feminism," reported on by Natalie Angier of the *New York Times*.

2. There has been some discussion about why it took biologists so long to recognize the specter of maternal certainty. Was it because most biologists are males and males are most concerned with looking at issues from the male point of view? Or was it that all biologists are humans, and humans are mammals, for whom there is never any question of who is the mother? Maternal certainty is, indeed, only a problem for egg-laying animals and only for those egg-laying animals that care for their eggs and young but must leave them on occasion to look for food or water, giving other females the opportunity to slip in and lay an egg. It is, in other words, mostly a bird problem.

3. This percentage may be somewhat low since it is easy to underestimate paternal care in mammals. Unlike maternal care, paternal care is not always obvious. The male elephant shrew of Africa, for example, spends considerable time maintaining a network of trails throughout the terri-

tory that he shares with his mate. He doesn't feed his young or carry them about or defend them against predators, but they benefit greatly from the many escape routes that he creates and from the foraging grounds that his trails make accessible.

4. Human males have been called "ecologically monogamous" because of their tendency to take more than one wife in those parts of the world where resources are abundant and where males, or some males at least, can accumulate or defend enough of those resources to support more than one family.

IV. THE ART OF NESTING

1. Officially, the Wildlife Conservation Park.

2. Termites are an entirely different order of insect, with their own reason for living in large social groups and for the wingless, sterile workers that tend the colony's young: inbreeding. A termite nest is founded by a single male and female that mate exclusively with each other (in the normal, diploid fashion) until one of them dies. The surviving partner then selects one of the offspring with which to continue mating. The end result is the same as in an ant's nest: siblings that are more closely related to each other than to any offspring they might have.

3. An exception, it would seem, are the kibbutzim of Israel. When the kibbutzim were first established in the early 1900s by immigrants from Russia, participants agreed to raise their children communally. Children were fed in the common dining room, and they slept in the "children's house." After just one generation, though, the system began to break down. Parents wanted more contact with their own offspring, and they wanted more time alone as families. They, like most humans, wanted a child-care system that was less communal.

4. Nests *are* also essential to the egg-laying mammals, the spiny anteater and the platypus. In a riverbank in southern Australia, the female platypus digs a long, sinuous tunnel with an underwater entrance. At the end of the tunnel (which can measure thirty feet), in a damp, grass-lined nest, she lays two soft-shelled eggs, which she then incubates for ten to twelve days by clutching them between her abdomen and tail. Each time she en-

ters her nest, she blocks the tunnel off with mud at intervals to protect against intruders and floods and to keep out the cold.

V. EGG LAYERS AND LIVE BIRTHERS

1. Egg order is not always the last word in survival, as researchers have recently found. Some birds, canaries, for instance, compensate for the inequities of asynchronous hatching by dosing their later-laid eggs with increasing amounts of the strength-giving hormone testosterone. In this way a canary's youngest chick is just as able to beg for food and demand parental attention as the oldest one. Researchers do not know yet how widespread this phenomenon is among birds, but it may be an adaptation on the part of some birds to a change in food supply toward greater predictability and stability.

2. This probability exists for most animals because it produces the most stable results. To understand this, imagine what would happen if a certain population of animals started preferentially producing offspring of one sex, males, for instance. When those male offspring grew up and began looking around for mates, they would have a hard time finding them. All the female offspring, but only some of the males, would be able to mate. So the parents that specialized in males would wind up having fewer grandchildren than those that produced females. If too many parents then began to specialize in daughters, the same thing would happen, and the surplus of daughters would lead to advantages for those parents that produced sons. Over time, as the respected mathematician Ronald Fisher reasoned, the pendulum may swing back and forth, but it will eventually settle on the probability that gives parents the best shot at grandchildren and great-grandchildren: fifty-fifty. This is Fisher's theorem of sex ratios, and it applies as long as there is little inbreeding in a population and as long as all individuals have the same opportunities to breed, conditions that Trivers and Willard realized do not always exist.

3. These astonishing findings beg the question, of course, of whether this kind of sex biasing could occur in human populations. Trivers and Willard suggested that it could, in populations that are differentiated on a socioeconomic scale where females tend to marry males of a higher socioeconomic status. In their paper they cited statistics indicating that wealthy Americans produce more sons than daughters. Their assertions

that humans can, at some unconscious level, skew the sex of their off-spring are still being debated, but in many societies, of course, boys are given conscious preferential treatment before and after birth. Girls are selectively aborted in many countries and are much more frequently abandoned or killed after birth. Boys are nursed longer by their mothers and coddled in subtle and not so subtle ways.

VI. BIRTH AND HATCHING — EMERGENCE

1. Humans differ from other primates in this regard, for with the exception of some New Age parents, mothers all over the world do not eat the placenta after delivery. In many cultures, though, the placenta is thought to have an important spiritual connection with the newborn and is prepared in special ways and buried.

2. John Bowlby leapt from geese to humans in formulating his attachment theory, but the reason his leap was successful was that Bowlby saw a similar behavior in geese and humans—separation anxiety—and proposed that it might have a similar cause. Klaus and Kennell did not actually observe similar behavior in sheep and humans, yet they hypothesized that it exists.

VII. WHOSE CHILD IS THIS?

1. One might think that such a high rate of parasitism would have led to counteradaptations, and it has. In most birds that live in large colonies, males follow their mates wherever they go in order to prevent rivals from copulating with them. Among cliff swallows, however, males guard their nests instead of their mates. The risk of egg dumping, it seems, is greater than that of cuckoldry. It is only when males leave their nests, for whatever reason, that eggs are dumped or transferred into them.

2. Another example of how genetic information is changing scientists' views of altruistic behavior like adoption and communal care is avian adoption. In some bird species, eastern bluebirds included, males have been known to adopt the brood of a female who has lost her mate. The male's behavior, it used to be thought, gave him access to the female when it came time to renest, and in this view adoption was an alternative to the infanticide practiced by the males of other bird species. It was thought to be the pre-

ferred strategy in species like the bluebird which raises two clutches in one season and which break the pair bond and disperse following nest failure. If the adoptive male helps the female to succeed with her first brood, the theory went, she will stick around and raise a brood with him. But now that ornithologists know about the frequency of extrapair copulation in the bird world, many think that the adoptive father has baser motives for behaving as he does, that he has reason to believe that at least part of the brood is his.

Male rodents use similar cues for deciding whether to tolerate or kill a nest full of young rodents. Males tolerate the pups if they have copulated with the mother and kill the pups if they have not. It is interesting that these males respond in the same way even when the pups have been exchanged at birth. They recognize offspring by their past sexual association with the mother, not by characteristics of the young themselves.

IX. THE EVOLUTION OF LOVE

1. I wonder if anyone can read the Altmanns' descriptions of high-ranking baboon infants—of Alice the Obnoxious, as one such infant was dubbed, who "spent much of her time with other mothers in the group, sitting in their laps and even pushing their infants aside in order to make room for herself"—without thinking of the high-ranking children of our own society: the Kennedy children who rode their ponies through their neighbors' gardens, or Nelson Rockefeller's son who was always allowed to interrupt his father's meetings.

2. These results bear an awful similarity to the results that Harlow got when he raised rhesus monkey infants on punitive surrogate mothers, which delivered blasts of compressed air during the time the infants spent in contact with them. The infants spent more time on these "rejecting mothers" than did control infants raised on the standard nonpunitive, cloth surrogates.

3. Dr. Kerstin Uvnas-Moberg presented her findings at a conference called "The Integrative Neurobiology of Affiliation" held at Georgetown University in April 1996.

X. THE LIMITS OF DEVOTION

1. Countrywomen developed an inexpensive alternative to wet nurses: personal goats. As the sixteenth-century French essayist Michel de Montaigne observed, "It is ordinary around where I live to see village women, when they cannot feed their children from their breasts, call goats to their aid; and I have at this moment two lackeys who never sucked women's milk for more than a week. These goats are promptly trained to come and suckle these little children; they recognize their voices when they call out, and come running. If any other than their nursling is presented to them, they refuse it; and the child does the same with another goat. I saw one the other day whose goat they took away because his father had only borrowed her from a neighbor of his; he never could take to the other that they presented to him, and doubtless died of hunger." Montaigne concluded that "animals alter and corrupt their natural affection as easily as we," but the vignette also shows how willing mothers are to shunt the costs of parental care and lactation when they can. I have not been able to find out how common the use of goats was, but I suspect that it is no small coincidence that Nanny is the name for both a female goat and a child's nurse.

Bibliography

Ainsworth, Mary D. Salter, and Bowlby, John. "An Ethological Approach to Personality Development." *American Psychologist* 46 (1991): 333–341.

Alcock, John. "Father Knows Best." *Natural History* 2 (1988): 20–22.

Altmann, J., S. A. Altmann, and G. Hausfater. 1978. "Primate Infant's Effects on Mother's Future Reproduction." *Science* 201 (1978): 1028–1030.

Altmann, J., G. Hausfater, and S. A. Altmann. "Determinants of Reproductive Success in Savannah Baboons." In T. H. Clutton-Brock, ed., *Reproductive Success.* Chicago: University of Chicago Press, 1988.

Angier, Natalie. "Canary Chicks: Not All Created Equal." *New York Times,* January 25, 1994, C-1, C-8.

———. "Feminists and Darwin: Scientists Try Closing the Gap." *New York Times,* June 21, 1994, C-1, C-13.

———. "Mother's Milk Found to Be Potent Cocktail of Hormones." *New York Times,* May 24, 1994, C-1, C-10.

Ar, A., and Yom-Tov, Y. "The Evolution of Parental Care in Birds." *Evolution* 32 (1978): 655–669.

Arney, William Ray. "Maternal-Infant Bonding: The Politics of Falling in Love with Your Child." *Feminist Studies* 6 (1980): 547–570.

Ashcroft, Gregory E. W. "Attempted Defense of a Lamb by a Female Bighorn Sheep." *Journal of Mammology* 67 (1986): 427–428.

Austin, C. R., and Short, R. V., eds. *Reproduction in Mammals,* vol. 4. Cambridge: Cambridge University Press, 1984.

Bell, Silvia M., and Ainsworth, Mary D. Salter. "Infant Crying and Maternal Responsiveness." *Child Development* 43 (1972): 1171–90.

Ben Shaul, Devorah Miller. "The Composition of the Milk of Wild Animals." *International Zoology Yearbook* 4 (1962): 333–342.

Berger, Joel. "Pregnancy Incentives, Predation Constraints and Habitat Shifts: Experimental and Field Evidence for Wild Bighorn Sheep." *Animal Behaviour* 41 (1991): 61–77.

Birkhead, Tim. *Great Auk Islands: A Field Biologist in the Arctic.* London: T. and A. D. Poyser, 1993.

Blackburn, Daniel G., and Evans, Howard E. "Why Are There No Viviparous Birds?" *American Naturalist* 128 (1986): 165–190.

Blass, Elliott M., and Teicher, Martin H. "Suckling." *Science* 210 (1980): 15–22.

Bleichfeld, Bruce, and Moely, Barbara E. "Psychophysiological Responses to an Infant Cry: Comparison of Groups of Women in Different Phases of the Maternal Cycle." *Developmental Psychology* 20 (1984): 1082–91.

Blurton Jones, Nicholas, ed. *Ethological Studies of Child Behaviour.* Cambridge: Cambridge University Press, 1972.

Bowlby, John. *Attachment and Loss,* vol. 1, *Attachment.* New York: Basic Books, 1969.

———. "The Nature of the Child's Tie to His Mother." *International Journal of Psycho-analysis* 39 (1958): 350–373.

Bretherton, Inge. "The Origins of Attachment Theory: John Bowlby and Mary Ainsworth." *Developmental Psychology* 28 (1992): 759–775.

Brockman, H. Jane. "Father of the Brood." *Natural History* 7 (1988): 33–36.

Brown, Charles R. "Cliff Swallow Colonies as Information Centers." *Science* 234 (1986): 83–85.

Brown, Charles R., and Brown, Mary Bomberger. "The Great Egg Scramble." *Natural History* 2 (1990): 34–40.

———. "A New Form of Reproductive Parasitism in Cliff Swallows." *Nature* 331 (1988): 66–67.

Browne, Malcome, W. "Eggs on Feet and Far from Shelter, Male Penguins Do a Shuffle." *New York Times,* September 27, 1994, C-1, C-14.

Bruemmer, Fred. "Survival of the Fattest." *Natural History* 7 (1990): 26–32.

Carey, Cynthia. "Structure and Function of Avian Eggs." *Current Ornithology* 1 (1983): 69–103.

Challinor, David. "Nature's Midwives and Nursemaids." *New Scientist* 1 (1983): 641.

Chappell, Mark A., Janes, Donald N., Shoemaker, Vaughan H., Bucher, Theresa L., and Maloney, Shane K. "Reproductive Effort in Adélie Penguins." *Behavioral Ecology and Sociobiology* 33 (1993): 173–182.

Clark, Anne Barrett, and Wilson, David Sloan. "Avian Breeding Adaptations: Hatching Asynchrony, Brood Reduction and Nest Failure." *Quarterly Review of Biology* 56 (1981): 253–275.

Clark, L., and Mason, J. Russell. "Use of Nest Material as Insecticidal and Anti-Pathogenic Agents by the European Starling." *Oecologia* (Berlin) 67 (1985): 169–176.

Clutton-Brock, T. H. *The Evolution of Parental Care.* Princeton: Princeton University Press, 1991.

Clutton-Brock, Tim. "The Red Deer of Rhum." *Natural History* 11 (1982): 43–46.

Clutton-Brock, T. H., Albon, S. D., and Guinness, F. E. "Reproductive Success in Red Deer." In T. H. Clutton-Brock, ed., *Reproductive Success.* Chicago: University of Chicago Press, 1988.

Collias, Nicholas E. "The Analysis of Socialization in Sheep and Goats." *Ecology* 37 (1956): 228–239.

Collias, Nicholas E., and Collias, Elsie C. *Evolution of Nest-Building in the Weaverbirds.* Berkeley and Los Angeles: University of California Press, 1964.

————. *Nest Building and Bird Behavior.* Princeton: Princeton University Press, 1984.

Collopy, Michael W. "Parental Care and Feeding Ecology of Golden Eagle Nestlings." *Auk* 101 (1984): 753–760.

Corben, C. J., Ingram, G. J., and Tyler, M. J. "Gastric Brooding: Unique Form of Parental Care in an Australian Frog." *Science* 186 (1974): 946–947.

Daly, Martin. "Why Don't Male Mammals Lactate?" *Journal of Theoretical Biology* 78 (1979): 325–345.

Davies, Nicholas B. *Dunnock Behaviour and Social Evolution.* Oxford: Oxford University Press, 1992.

Dawkins, Richard. *The Selfish Gene.* Oxford: Oxford University Press, 1976.

Dixon, Charles. *Birds' Nests: An Introduction to the Science of Caliology.* New York: Frederick A. Stokes, 1902.

Doty, R. L. "Odor-Guided Behavior in Mammals." *Experientia* 42 (1986): 257–271.

Dunbar, Robin. "Monogamy on the Rocks." *Natural History* 11 (1985): 41–46.

Ember, Melvin, and Ember, Carol R. "Male-Female Bonding: A Cross-Species Study of Mammals and Birds." *Behavior Science Research* 1 (1979): 37–56.

Evans, Howard E., and O'Neill, Kevin M. "Beewolves." *Scientific American* 265 (1991): 70–76.

Feldman, Hillary N. "Maternal Care and Differences in the Use of Nests in the Domestic Cat." *Animal Behaviour* 45 (1993): 13–23.

Fisher, Helen E. *Anatomy of Love: The Natural History of Monogamy, Adultery and Divorce.* New York: W. W. Norton, 1992.

Fisher, Ronald A. *The Genetical Theory of Natural Selection.* Oxford, England: Oxford University Press, 1930.

Fleming, Alison S., and Corter, Carl. "Factors Influencing Maternal Responsiveness in Humans: Usefulness of an Animal Model." *Psychoneuroendocrinology* 13 (1988): 189–212.

Francis, Charles M., Anthony, Edythe L. P., Brunton, Jennifer A., and Kunz, Thomas H. "Lactation in Male Fruit Bats." *Nature* 367 (1994): 691–692.

Freedman, Daniel G. "Ethnic Differences in Babies." *Human Nature,* January 1979, 36–43.

―――. *Human Infancy: An Evolutionary Perspective.* Hillsdale, N.J.: Lawrence Erlbaum, 1974.

Gaston, A. J., Cairns, D. K., Elliot, R. D., and Noble, D. G. *A Natural History of Digges Sound.* Ottawa: Canadian Wildlife Service Report Series 46, 1985.

Gaston, A. J., and Nettleship, David. *The Thick-Billed Murres of Prince Leopold Island.* Ottawa: Canadian Wildlife Service Monograph Series 6, 1981.

Gaston, Tony. "Down to the Sea." *Natural History* 7 (1988): 26–28.

―――. "Seabird Citadels of the Arctic." *Natural History* 4(1987): 54–58.

Gaulin, Steven J. C., and Schlegel, Alice. "Paternal Confidence and Paternal Investment: A Cross-Cultural Test of a Sociobiological Hypothesis." *Ethology and Sociobiology* 1 (1980): 301–309.

Gehlbach, F. R., and Baldridge, R. S. "Live Blind Snakes *(Leptotyphlops dulcis)* in Eastern Screech Owl *(Otus asio)* Nests: A Novel Commensalism." *Oecologia* (Berlin) 71 (1987): 560–563.

Goldberg, Susan. "Parent-Infant Bonding: Another Look." *Child Development* 54 (1983): 1355–82.

Goodall, Jane, and Athumani, Jumanne. "An Observed Birth in a Free-Living Chimpanzee *(Pan troglodytes schweinfurthii)* in Gombe National Park, Tanzania." *Primates* 21 (1980): 545–549.

Gowaty, Patricia Adair. "Bluebird Belligerence." *Natural History* 6 (1985): 8–12.

Gowaty, Patricia Adair, Plissner, Jonathan H., and Williams, Tracey G. "Behavioural Correlates of Uncertain Parentage: Mate Guarding and Nest Guarding by Eastern Bluebirds, *Sialia sialis."* *Animal Behaviour* 38 (1989): 272–284.

Gubernick, David J., and Klopfer, Peter H. *Parental Care in Mammals.* New York: Plenum Press, 1981.

Halls, Lowell K., ed. *White-Tailed Deer—Ecology and Management.* Harrisburg, Pa.: Stackpole, 1984.

Hamilton, W. D. "Geometry for the Selfish Herd." *Journal of Theoretical Biology* 31 (1971): 295–311.

Hansell, Michael H. *Animal Architecture and Building Behavior.* London: Longman, 1984.

———. "Wasp Papier-mâché." *Natural History* 8 (1989): 52–61.

Harlow, Harry F. "The Nature of Love." *American Psychologist* 13 (1958): 673–685.

Harlow, Harry F., and Harlow, Margaret K. "The Affectional Systems." In *Behavior of Nonhuman Primates,* vol. 2, Allan M. Schrier, Harry F. Harlow, and Fred Stollnitz, eds. New York: Academic Press, 1965.

Harvey, Paul H., Read, Andrew F., and Promislow, Daniel E. L. "Life History Variation in Placental Mammals: Unifying the Data with Theory." *Oxford Surveys in Evolutionary Biology* 6 (1989): 13–31.

Headstrom, Richard. *A Complete Field Guide to Nests in the United States.* New York: Ives Washburn, 1970.

Heinrich, Bernd. "Why Is a Robin's Egg Blue?" *Audubon,* July 1986, 65–71.

Hensley, R. Craig, and Smith, Kimberly G. "Eastern Bluebird Responses to Nocturnal Black Rat Snake Nest Predation." *Wilson Bulletin* 98 (1986): 602–603.

Hill, Kim. "Life History Theory and Evolutionary Anthropology." *Evolutionary Anthropology* 2 (1993): 78–88.

Hinde, Robert A., and Hinde, Joan Stevenson. "Attachment: Biological, Cultural and Individual Desiderata." *Human Development* 33 (1990): 62–72.

Holldobler, Bert, and Wilson, Edward O. *Journey to the Ants.* Cambridge: Belknap Press, Harvard University Press, 1994.

Howrigan, Gail A. "Fertility, Infant Feeding, and Change in Yucatán." *New Directions for Child Development* 40 (1988): 37–50.

Hrdy, Sarah Blaffer. "Daughters or Sons." *Natural History* 4 (1988): 64–83.

Janson, Charles H. "Capuchin Counterpoint." *Natural History* 2 (1986): 45–52.

Kay, Margarita Artschwager. *Anthropology of Human Birth.* Philadelphia: F. A. Davis, 1982.

Klaus, Marshall H., and Kennell, John H. *Maternal-Infant Bonding.* St. Louis: C. V. Mosby, 1976.

Klaus, Marshall H., Kennell, John H., Plumb, Nancy, and Zuehlke, Steven. "Human Maternal Behavior at the First Contact with Her Young." *Pediatrics* 46 (1970): 187–192.

Klopfer, Peter H. "Mother Love: What Turns It On?" *American Scientist* 59 (1971): 404–407.

Konner, Melvin. "Biological Aspects of the Mother-Infant Bond." In *The Development of Attachment and Affiliative Systems,* Robert N. Emde and Robert J. Harmon, eds. New York: Plenum Press, 1982.

———. *Childhood.* Boston: Little, Brown, 1991.

———. "Evolution of Human Behavior Development." In *Culture and Infancy Variations in the Human Experience,* P. Herbert Leiderman, Steven R. Tulkin, and Anne Rosenfeld, eds. New York: Academic Press, 1977.

Lack, David. *Ecological Adaptations for Breeding in Birds.* London: Methuen, 1968.

———. "The Significance of Clutch-Size." *Ibis* 89 (1947): 302–352.

Lamb, Michael E. "Early Mother-Neonate Contact and the Mother-Child Relationship." *Journal of Child Psychology* 24 (1983): 487–494.

Lancaster, Jane B., Altmann, Jeanne, Rossi, Alice S., and Sherrod, Lonnie R., eds. *Parenting Across the Life Span.* New York: Aldine de Gruyter, 1987.

Lancaster, Jane B., and Lancaster, Chet S. "Parental Investment: The Hominid Adaptation." In *How Humans Adapt: A Biocultural Odyssey,* Donald J. Ortner, ed. Washington, D.C.: Smithsonian Institution Press, 1983.

Lawrence, Alistair B. "Mother-Daughter and Peer Relationship of Scottish Hill Sheep." *Animal Behaviour* 39 (1990): 481–486.

Leach, Penelope. *Babyhood.* New York: Alfred A. Knopf, 1976.

Lee, Richard B. "Lactation, Ovulation, Infanticide, and Women's Work: A Study of Hunter-Gatherer Population Regulation." In *Biosocial Mechanisms of Population Regulation,* Mark Nathan Cohen, Roy S. Malpass, and Harold G. Klein, eds. New Haven: Yale University Press, 1980.

Leiderman, P. Herbert, Tulkin, Steven R., and Rosenfeld, Anne. *Culture and Infancy: Variations in the Human Experience.* New York: Academic Press, 1977.

LeVine, Robert A. "Human Parental Care: Universal Goals, Cultural Strategies, Individual Behavior." *New Directions for Child Development* 40 (1988): 3–11.

LeVine, R. A. "Parental Goals: A Cross-Cultural View." *Teachers College Record* 76 (1974): 226–239.

Levy, F., and Poindron, P. "The Importance of Amniotic Fluids for the Establishment of Maternal Behaviour in Experienced and Inexperienced Ewes." *Animal Behaviour* 35 (1987): 1188–92.

Lewin, Roger. "Egglaying Is for the Birds." *Research News* 46 (1986): 285.

Luft, Joan, and Altmann, Jeanne. "Mother Baboon." *Natural History* 9 (1982): 31–38.

Lyderson, Christian, and Ryg, Morten. "Evaluating Breeding Habitat and Populations of Ringed Seals *Phoca hispida* in Svalbard Fjords." *Polar Record* 27 (1991): 223–228.

McCracken, Gary F., and Gustin, Mary K. "Batmom's Daily Nightmare." *Natural History* 10 (1987): 66–72.

Makin, Jennifer W., and Porter, Richard H. "Attractiveness of Lactating Females' Breast Odors to Neonates." *Child Development* 60 (1989): 803–810.

Malaurie, Jean. *The Last Kings of Thule.* Chicago: University of Chicago Press: 1982.

Marchant, R. A. *Where Animals Live.* New York: Macmillan, 1970.

Maurer, Daphne, and Maurer, Charles. *The World of the Newborn.* New York: Basic Books, 1988.

Maynard Smith, John. "Evolution and the Theory of Games." *American Scientist* 64 (1976): 141–145.

―――. "The Theory of Games and the Evolution of Animal Conflict," *Journal of Theoretical Biology* 47 (1974): 209–221.

Meek, Susan B., and Robertson, Raleigh J. "Adoption of Young by Replacement Male Birds: An Experimental Study of Eastern Bluebirds and a Review." *Animal Behaviour* 42 (1991): 813–820.

Montaigne, Michel de. *The Complete Works of Montaigne.* Trans. Donald M. Frame. Stanford: Stanford University Press, 1958.

Mull, Dorothy S. "Mother's Milk and Pseudoscientific Breastmilk Testing in Pakistan." *Social Science Medicine* 34 (1992): 1277–90.

Myers, Barbara J. "Mother-Infant Bonding: The Status of the Critical-Period Hypothesis." *Developmental Review* 4 (1984): 240–274.

Nowak, R. "Senses Involved in Discrimination of Merino Ewes at Close Contact and from a Distance by Their Newborn Lambs." *Animal Behaviour* 42 (1991): 357–366.

Parker, Malcolm, ed. *Comparative Aspects of Lactation.* Symposia of the Zoological Society of London, no. 41. London: Academic Press, 1977.

Pederson, Patricia E., and Blass, Elliott M. "Prenatal and Postnatal Determinants of the First Suckling Episode in Albino Rats." *Developmental Psychobiology* 15 (1982): 349–355.

Perrone, Michael, Jr., and Zaret, Thomas M. "Parental Care Patterns of Fishes." *American Naturalist* 113 (1979): 351–361.

Pinkowski, Benedict D. "A Comparative Study of the Behavioral and Breeding Ecology of the Eastern Bluebird." Ph.D. diss., Wayne State University, 1974.

Pond, Caroline M. "The Significance of Lactation in the Evolution of Mammals." *Evolution* 31 (1977): 177–199.

Porter, Richard H. "Human Reproduction and the Mother-Infant Relationship: The Role of Odors." In *Smell and Taste in Health and Disease,* Thomas V. Getchell, Richard L. Doty, Linda M. Bartoshuk, and James B. Snow, Jr., eds. New York: Raven Press, 1991.

Porter, Richard H., Makin, Jennifer W., Davis, Linda B., and Christensen, Katherine M. "Breast-fed Infants Respond to Olfactory Cues from Their Own Mother and Unfamiliar Lactating Females." *Infant Behavior and Development* 15 (1992): 85–93.

Pryce, C. R. "A Comparative Systems Model of the Regulation of Maternal Motivation in Mammals." *Animal Behaviour* 43 (1992): 417–441.

Rheingold, Harriet Lange. *Maternal Behavior in Mammals.* New York: John Wiley, 1963.

Richman, Amy L., LeVine, Robert A., New, Rebecca Staples, Howrigan, Gail A., Welles-Nysrom, Barbara, and LeVine, Sarah E. "Maternal Behavior to Infants in Five Cultures." *New Directions for Child Development* 40 (1988): 81–97.

Ridley, Matt. *The Red Queen: Sex and the Evolution of Human Nature.* New York: Macmillan, 1994.

Riedman, Marianne L. "The Evolution of Alloparental Care and Adoption in Mammals and Birds." *Quarterly Review of Biology* 57 (1982): 405–435.

Rossi, Alice S. "Gender and Parenthood." *American Sociological Review* 49 (1984): 1–19.

Rowell, T. E. "Till Death Us Do Part: Long-Lasting Bonds Between Ewes and Their Daughters." *Animal Behaviour* 42 (1991): 681–682.

Rubenstein, Daniel I., and Wrangham, Richard W., eds. *Ecological Aspects of Social Evolution.* Princeton: Princeton University Press, 1986.

Russel, Michael J., Mendelson, Terrie, and Peeke, Harmon V. S. "Mothers' Identification of Their Infants' Odors." *Ethology and Sociobiology* 4 (1983): 29–31.

Sagi, Abraham. "Attachment Theory and Research from a Cross-Cultural Perspective." *Human Development* 33 (1990): 10–22.

Schaller, George B. *The Serengeti Lion: A Study of Predator-Prey Relations.* Chicago: University of Chicago Press, 1972.

Schwede, George, Hendrichs, Hubert, and McShea, William. "Social and Spatial Organization of Female White-Tailed Deer, *Odocoileus virginianus,* During the Fawning Season." *Animal Behaviour* 45 (1993) 1007–17.

Scott, Michelle Pellissier, and Traniello, James F. A. "Guardians of the Underworld." *Natural History* 6 (1989): 33–36.

Shine, Richard. "Parental Care in Reptiles." In *Biology of the Reptilia,* vol. 16, *Defense and Life History,* Carl Gans, ed. New York: Alan R. Liss, 1988.

Short, R. V. "Breast Feeding." *Scientific American* 250 (1984): 35–43.

Skutch, Alexander F. *Parent Birds and Their Young.* Austin: University of Texas Press, 1976.

Sluckin, Wladyslaw, and Herbert, Martin. *Parental Behaviour.* Oxford: Basil Blackwell, 1986.

Standon, V., and Foley, R. A., eds. *Comparative Socioecology: The Behavioural Ecology of Humans and Other Mammals* (Special Publication 8 of the British Ecological Society). Oxford: Blackwell, 1989.

Suomi, S. "Abnormal Behavior and Primate Models of Psychopathology." In *Primate Behavior,* J. Fobes and J. King, eds. New York: Academic Press, 1982.

Sussman, George D. "Parisian Infants and Norman Wet Nurses in the Early Nineteenth Century: A Statistical Study." *Journal of Interdisciplinary History* 7 (1977): 637–653.

Takahashi, Keiko. "Are the Key Assumptions of the 'Strange Situation' Procedure Universal? A View from Japanese Research." *Human Development* 33 (1990): 23–30.

Taylor, Brent, and Wadsworth, Jane. "Breast Feeding and Child Development at Five Years." *Developmental Medicine and Child Neurology* 26 (1984): 73–80.

Terborgh, John, and Goldizen, Ann Wilson. "On the Mating System of the Cooperatively Breeding Saddle-Backed Tamarin *(Saguinus fuscicollis).*" *Behavioral Ecology and Sociobiology* 16 (1985): 293–299.

Thomas, Elizabeth Marshall. *The Harmless People.* New York: Alfred A. Knopf, 1958.

Townsend, Daniel S. "Fatherhood in Frogdom." *Natural History* 5 (1987): 28–34.

Trevathan, Wenda R. *Human Birth: An Evolutionary Perspective.* New York: Aldine de Gruyter, 1987.

Trivers, Robert L. "The Evolution of Reciprocal Altruism." *Quarterly Review of Biology* 46 (1971): 35–57.

———. "Parental Investment and Sexual Selection." In *Sexual Selection and the Descent of Man,* B. Campbell, ed. Chicago: Aldine, 1972.

———. "Parent-Offspring Conflict." *American Zoologist* 14 (1974): 249–264.

———. *Social Evolution.* Menlo Park, Calif.: Benjamin Cummings, 1985.

Trivers, R. L., and Hare, H. "Haplodiploidy and the Evolution of the Social Insects." *Science* 191 (1976): 249–263.

Trivers, Robert L., and Willard, Dan E. "Natural Selection of Parental Ability to Vary the Sex Ratio of Offspring." *Science* 179 (1973): 90–92.

van Ijzendoorn, Marinus H. "Developments in Cross-Cultural Research on Attachment: Some Methodological Notes." *Human Development* 33 (1990): 3–9.

van Lawick Goodall, Jane. *In the Shadow of Man.* Boston: Houghton Mifflin, 1971.

Vince, Margaret A., and Ward, T. M. "The Responsiveness of Newly Born Clun Forest Lambs to Odour Sources in the Ewe." *Behaviour* 89 (1984): 117–127.

Vince, Margaret A., Ward, T. M., and Reader, Margaret. "Tactile Stimulation and Teat-Seeking Behaviour in Newly Born Lambs." *Animal Behaviour* 32 (1984): 1179–84.

Vincent, Amanda. "A Seahorse Father Makes a Good Mother." *Natural History* 12 (1990): 34–43.

von Frisch, Karl. *Animal Architecture.* New York: Harcourt Brace Jovanovich, 1974.

White, Fred N., and Kinney, James L. "Avian Incubation." *Science* 186 (1974): 107–115.

Wilson, Edward O. *Naturalist.* Washington, D.C.: Island Press, 1994.

————. *Sociobiology: The New Synthesis.* Cambridge: Belknap Press, Harvard University Press, 1975.

Wimberger, Peter H. "The Use of Green Plant Material in Bird Nests to Avoid Ectoparasites." *Auk* 101 (1984): 615–618.

Wright, Lawrence. "Double Mystery." *New Yorker,* August 7, 1995, 44–62.

Wright, Peter. "Learning Experiences in Feeding Behaviour During Infancy." *Journal of Psychosomatic Research* 32 (1988): 613–619.

Wright, Robert. *The Moral Animal.* New York: Pantheon, 1994.

Zeveloff, Samuel I., and Boyce, Mark S. "Parental Investment and Mating Systems in Mammals." *Evolution* 34 (1980): 973–982.

————. "Why Human Neonates Are So Altricial." *American Naturalist* 120 (1982): 537–542.

Index

About the Author

Susan Allport is a writer specializing in history and science. Her books include *Sermons in Stone: The Stone Walls of New England and New York* and *Explorers of the Black Box: The Search for the Cellular Basis of Memory*. Allport has contributed essays, travel articles, and other pieces to the *New York Times,* the *International Herald Tribune,* the *Hartford Courant, Audubon, Connoisseur,* the *Providence Journal-Bulletin,* and the *Missouri Review.* She lives with her husband and two children in Katonah, New York.

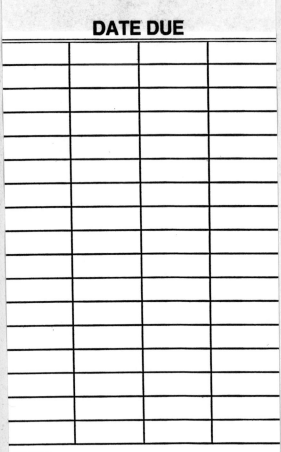

DATE DUE

FOLLETT